HUMAN IDENTITY
through
Scientific, Philosophical and Artistic Concepts in the Quran

Shams Un Nahar Zaman

AuthorHouse™ UK Ltd.
500 Avebury Boulevard
Central Milton Keynes, MK9 2BE
www.authorhouse.co.uk
Phone: 08001974150

© 2009 Shams Un Nahar Zaman. All rights reserved.

No part of this book may be reproduced, stored in a retrieval system, or transmitted by any means without the written permission of the author.

First published by AuthorHouse 6/8/2009

ISBN: 978-1-4389-6931-2 (sc)
ISBN: 978-1-4389-6930-5 (hc)

Printed in the United States of America
Bloomington, Indiana

This book is printed on acid-free paper.

ACKNOWLEDGEMENTS

I thank my family members, including my husband, Professor Q. A. M. Zaman, and my brothers, Dr M. Zahir and M. Zamir, who always encouraged and gave me many valuable suggestions.

My grandson Misbah helped to format a table that had become difficult for me to finish, and I thank him for that. Continuous joyous encouragements from all my grandchildren helped to finalise this work.

My daughters Rumana Zuberi, Maher Anjum and Muna Anjum gave valuable time out of their heavy daily schedule to read and help in writing and drafting the manuscript. Their critical and constructive comments and observations produced the final version of this book.

Finally, it is up to the reader to judge whether or not this book provides a stimulus for discussion. All ideas are my own and only I take the responsibility for the concepts in this book. This work was created in the hope that it would provoke a renewed interest in understanding the Quran from a contemporary perspective and by our younger generations. This book is neither a theological nor a sociological discourse but rather an attempt to establish a global human identity.

Shams N. Zaman
July 2008

I dedicate this book in memory of my parents, Justice Muhammad Asir and
Begum Husne Ara Asir, who trained my mind to look beyond the horizon.

PREFACE

All ideas discussed in this book are based on my talks delivered at various institutions in the United Kingdom between 1996 and 2003. The Quran has always fascinated me in the variety of its style, philosophies and subjects. I have tried to understand the Quran through my exploration of science, philosophy and the arts. Similarly, I have regularly taken a keen interest in the physical, moral and aesthetic features of human nature. Consequently, in this book I have interpreted Quranic ideas and concepts in the light of modern scientific, philosophical and artistic views. The central question underlying my search has always been what makes us human – that is to say, who are we? The Quranic passages that I have attempted to explain are presented in bold, with the sura and verse given for reference within brackets. For instance, (2.3) means the passage is from sura or chapter 2, verse 3. In a similar manner, all biblical passages are cited within brackets with the chapter and verse given, e.g. (Exod. 23.10).

Shams Zaman
August 2008
London

Abbreviation: (S:) *Sallallahu alaihe wassaallam*/May Allah's peace be upon him

Contents

INTRODUCTION	1
THE QURAN	8
Chapter One	13
Chapter Two	42
Chapter Three	73
Chapter Four	98
Chapter Five	130
Conclusion	169
References	171
List of Further Reading	173
Bibliography	175
Index	198

INTRODUCTION

The Quran presents a basis for theological discussions and offers a way of life for its followers. The Quranic narration on the identity of human life starts at the embryonic stage and continues through different phases of physical, social, philosophical and spiritual maturity. Although Prophet Muhammad (S:) used Arabic to convey his message, the author believes that the Quranic philosophies relate not only to Arabs but also to other communities of the world.

This book is an attempt to understand and interpret human identity through revelations found in the Quran. The Quran's aim is to encourage a person to reach philosophical and spiritual maturity and its revelations are addressed to a human mind that is assumed to be sensible and moderate. However, since the Quran was revealed fourteen hundred years ago, some might consider time to be a barrier to interpreting its meanings today. Critics may ask whether it is possible to assess and identify from the Quranic era human attributes that apply to all ages of mankind. The author hopes to address this issue in this book.

The main issue in establishing human identity according to the prevailing wisdom is to develop a sense of self in an individual [1][2], specifying 'who' or 'what' that person is. Although time is forever changing and moving forward [3][4], it also acts as a tool for assessing human life. For example, within the lifetime of a man or a woman the culture and knowledge of that contemporaneous age, which are constantly changing with time [5][6], will be the defining feature of that person. In other words, as Fritjof Capra [7] quoted from the I Ching, 'The old is discarded and the new is introduced'. Therefore, the frontiers of human knowledge and understanding are constantly changing and advancing with time, connecting the past with the future through the present.

Time has been regarded in the Quran as the unit needed to understand mankind and the knowledge we have acquired. In the chapter 'Dahr' or 'Time' or 'Man' in the Quran we find the verse **'it is We Who have sent down the Quran to thee by stages'** (76.23). This implies that the revelations came as a gradual process over the twenty-three years after Muhammad (S:) became Prophet up until his death. Human life and knowledge might have been different in many ways from ours in sixth- and seventh-century Arabia, but many questions of behaviour, philosophy and spirituality addressed in the Quran are still relevant today. In other words, although the Quranic revelations came in an age that was historically different from the twenty-first century, in reality people who lived in that period experienced the same upheavals in life as we do today.

The objective of this book is to trace the relevance of modern life and knowledge through the Quran. Life even in this modern age is recognized as a transient and not a permanent phase. It has been proved through modern science that the human being is one of the few living creatures that is readily adaptable to changes arising from climatic, environmental and extreme political circumstances. Bearing this in mind, a review of the scientific, philosophical and artistic notions in the Quran will determine whether they can be interpreted in a contemporary way and so be relevant to readers today. Since the Quran is represented as the Book that shows the way of life amongst the faithful, it is assumed that the aspects of life that we value are present in the Quran in a timeless manner.

In today's society, especially in the Western world, it is becoming increasingly difficult to survive without scientific knowledge. Our lives are dependent on science in many ways because it not only helps with our daily existence but also advances our standard of living. However, although science improves our lifestyle through materialistic advances, it does not or cannot shape our identity unless we decide the way we use such tools. At the end of the day society perhaps needs to lean on something other than just science-based worldly advances to survive.

Philosophy, which is a study of the basic truth and principles of life and morals, can be taken as a guide to understand human behaviour. The philosophical approach to truth and life is not a modern idea and has been practised since time immemorial. It helps to explain the meaning of religion [8]. The common person generally accepts philosophical opinions from a 'guru' without much questioning, although intellectuals debate the value of such philosophies and their relevance to modern society. The main attribute of philosophical influences is that they provide a guideline for individuals on how to accept and endure life. The implementation of this guidance in a constructive manner through one's intent and actions, while balancing the guidelines in principle and in practice, would be the ideal situation for an individual.

While time plays an important role in the human mind, art or artefacts from any region could be taken as a primitive form of self-expression which has been preserved through time [9]. Art is often thought of as representing the artist's cultural status or the cultural and spiritual development of a community. Using this description, painting, sculpture, music, dance and poetry have always been an integral part of human life and society. The artistic inspirations within the Quran are thought to possess beauty in their style and language, as well as in the way they approach the human heart and mind.

It is time to think again. Muslims need a new direction for understanding the Quran which is suitable for the modern age. Mustafa Ceric, Reis-Ul-Ulama, the Grand Mufti of Bosnia-Herzegovina [10], asked all European Muslims to apply 'freedom of spirit and strength of mind' to rediscover the passion and cultural creativity of past Islamic civilizations. We the Muslims have to accept science, philosophy and art as knowledge created by Allah, and understand how they can be applied in the light of the Quran in the twenty-first century. Hence in this book the author will draw parallels between the Quranic and modern views on science, philosophy and art.

The main connection between these three areas, i.e. science, philosophy and arts, is that they each play a role in forming human identity. Scientific knowledge verifies the reality of matter and its existence, supporting our physical nature and material world. Philosophical knowledge establishes the basis of right and wrong in our society. Artistic knowledge expands our horizons and our concepts to the edge of aesthetic perception. The amalgamation of these ideas qualifies our perception of the Quranic idea of human identity, and this can be relevant even today.

In non-monotheistic cultures, human society often attributed an immortal status of 'supreme being' to powerful people or objects and symbols of nature and in return asked favours from them. During times of adversity such powers were called upon to help alleviate pain and sickness. Monotheistic religions such as Islam and its predecessors uprooted these ideas and declared that all powers originated only from One source and humans had to ask Him favours.

In Islam, faith or belief in one God developed from the very beginning with human identity. Prophet Abraham or Ibrahim (S:) was the founding messenger of the One God theory which is the basis of all three monotheistic faiths [11]: Judaism, Christianity and Islam (see Figure 1). At the time of Islam's advent in Arabia, its monotheistic predecessors, Judaism and Christianity, were firmly rooted in the Arab peninsula and in other areas around the Mediterranean coast. In fact all three Prophets, namely Abraham or Ibrahim (S:), Moses or Musa (S:) and Jesus or Isa (S:), are highly respected in the Quran. All Prophets from this region after Abraham acknowledged the existence of One God, and their community came to be known as **'one community'** (23.52, 53). The teachings from the monotheistic faiths included ideas such as: **'there is no other god but God'**; **'obey and love God'**; **'honour your parents'**; **'do not kill'** and **'do not steal'** (6.52; Exod. 20.12–14; Exod. 23.10).

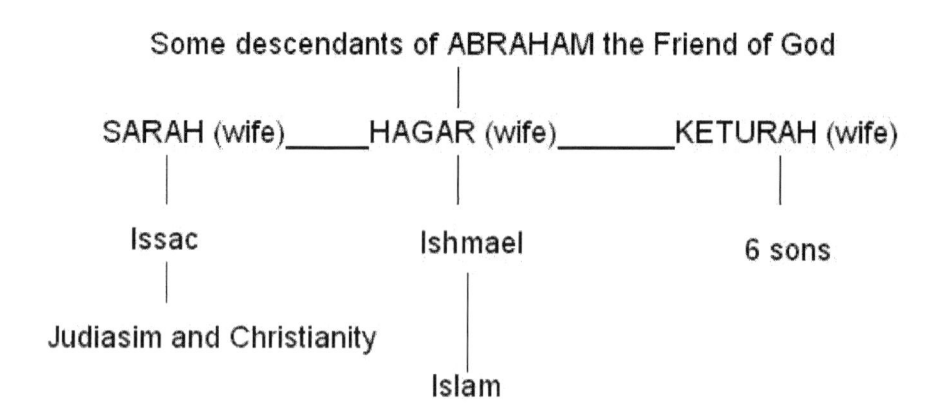

```
Some descendants of ABRAHAM the Friend of God
                              |
SARAH (wife)_____HAGAR (wife)_____KETURAH (wife)
    |                  |                    |
  Issac             Ishmael              6 sons
    |                  |
Judiasim and Christianity  |
                        Islam
```

Figure 1. Abraham's descendants (see ref 8)

Identity Through Science, Philosophy and Artistic Concepts in the Quran

William Dalrymple [12], in his article 'More a Family Falling Out than a Clash of Civilisations', wrote 'the links that bind Christianity, Judaism and Islam are so intricately woven that the more you learn about them, the more the occasional confrontations between them begin to seem like a civil war between different streams of the same tradition than any clash of civilizations'. It is essential therefore to have some elementary understanding of the connections between these three faiths. As we know, throughout the Middle East Prophet Abraham (S:) is still known as 'Ibrahim Khalilullah' or 'God's Friend'. People of these lands have a common cultural root and use similar words based on commonly spoken languages during the time when Judaism, Christianity and Islam were established in this area. For example, the word 'God' is represented as 'Elohim' or 'Yah' in Hebrew, 'Elah' in the Aramaic language and 'Allah' or 'Elahi' in Arabic [13] [14] [15].

At the beginning of the discussions in this book there is a short chapter on the Quran. It attempts to explain the background of the Quranic text. After the introductory chapter five more chapters explain the Quranic approach to human identity and spiritual development; knowledge and activity; relationships; the development of a philosophical guideline and the identification of a sense of aesthetics.

The Quran, according to F. Robinson [16], possesses a superhuman quality, even in its translation. Although in this book all references to religious scriptures are passages from the versions translated into English, some of the beauty of the original languages and styles may be lost. However, the author believes that in today's world translation and thereby accessibility is important because it allows greater understanding using a common platform. This is especially true in modern Britain because the population is now composed of many different cultures where English is the common language. In the Quran we find references to the use of a language that is understood by all: **'this book is given in your own language'** (13.37). Again, in another passage, the Quran stresses that God has **'created mankind with different colours, language and nationalities'** (10.19), thereby referring to multiculturism. Therefore we can conclude that at least in the UK today English translations ought to provide the best possible interpretation for all scriptures.

The first discussion chapter is 'Beginning: Islam and Medical

Science in the Light of the Quran'. The intention here is to point out that Islam is for people who care for an improved life both in this world and thereafter. Also, just as we accept that medicine brings physical relief, happiness and health to the patient, the Quran might provide self-recognition, mental stability and calmness.

'Limitation: Creation, Life and Activity' is the title of the second chapter, whichexplores three important ideas in our society through the Quran and science. Although science is a dynamic process of discovery and change, whereas the words of the Quran, which was revealed in the seventh century, have remained constant, in this book an attempt has been made to compare similar ideas from current scientific understandings and Quranic verses. The concept that time is a barrier to understanding and interpreting the Quran's knowledge on creation, life and activity is being challenged here by the author. In relation to activity, it is important to acknowledge that man's knowledge is limited owing to our mortal existence.

In the next chapter the discussion is entitled 'Relationships: Plants, Animals and the Human Species'. The main theme explored here is how the congenial relationships amongst plants, animals and humans might improve our identity and the well-being of this planet. As we are aware, humans are exploiting natural resources as commercial commodities, but is there still time to rectify our actions and curb our exploitations of these resources?

The fourth chapter discusses 'Philosophy: Unity and Diversity in Humans'. It looks at the hypothesis that although all humans belong to the same species we are not all identical in our thoughts and opinions. The previous chapters have related human identity to its physical, environmental and social interactions; while this chapter relates to similarities and differences that exist between members of communities, especially in relation to their understanding of good and bad, us and them. It is an attempt to relate Quranic verses with certain contemporary philosophy, faith and beliefs.

The last chapter, 'Fulfilment: Creative Art', explores the idea of art as represented in the Quranic philosophy. The Quran incorporates beauty and artistry that are revealed to the perceptive mind. According to its teachings everything in nature, as well as that produced through human inspirations, originates from God. So, can we consider God to be an artist? It is widely believed that artistic expressions, whether through poetry, music, painting or some other form, can provide fulfilment to the artist. The question remains whether accepting God as the ultimate artist can bring fulfilment to mankind.

In this book an analysis of the physical and spiritual nature of humans combined with an exploration of knowledge, activity, relationships and appreciation of beauty offers a unique opportunity to understand mankind.

THE QURAN

It is important to clarify that the Quranic verses were written down after they were revealed to the Prophet so that they would not be forgotten or lost. Significantly, the Prophet convinced his followers that **'understanding'** (39.18; 44.38, 39) the meaning of the revelations, rather than just reciting them, would make it easier for his followers to implement these ideas in their lives. This is because only a student of the Quran who has understood the truth will be able to accept that **'God's guidance comes with understanding'** (39.18; 44.38, 39) and will be in a position to apply these in practice.

The author believes that although the Quranic ideas and philosophy have remained constant it would be difficult to apply them in the twenty-first century in the same style and context as in sixth- and seventh-century Arabia. However, since in the Quran **'some of its verses are precise in meaning [,] they are the foundation of the Book – and others ambiguous no one but Allah has the correct meaning**' (3.7), it is possible to interpret the text to suit the time and historical context of the individual, and we can apply its teachings today as they were applied by our predecessors and will continue to be applied by our descendants. In this book a number of verses have been used more than once to explain a variety of Quranic concepts.

The question is: how do we interpret the Quran in our daily lives?

The Quran came with the simple message of one indivisible God to Muhammad (S:), who was declared to be the last Prophet, or messenger, by God. The Quran, with all its 114 chapters containing 6,235 verses [Y. Ali, 1978], should be understood with reference to a context. Generally, the following two approaches are used to understand their meaning:

I) By literal or direct transliteration. This explains the meaning of the verse in relation to the event that led to its revelation. So the meaning relates directly to the historical background as interpreted during the Prophet's revelation period.

II) By non-literal application. In this case the principle of the verses is applied to contemporary events. It can be applied to situations or events taking place at the present time which are comparable to Quranic references. The following verse supports this assertion: **'We have divided the Quran into sections so that you may recite it to the people with deliberation'** (17.106).

We know that the composition of the whole Quran was completed by Prophet Muhammad (S:) himself, and within twenty to twenty-five years of his death (AD 632) it was compiled in book form. The first thirteen years of the Quranic revelations were revealed in Makkah during times of adversity; this was followed by the Medina period after the Prophet's emigration there, a time of affluence when he played the role of a leader, a statesman and a philosopher. These two periods comprise the majority of the 114 suras. Both periods were then divided into the early, mid and late stages. In the third category suras were recognized as having been revealed in the mixed late Makkah and early Medina periods without any definite time or location identified. The fourth category comprises verses for which no exact time or historical origin is known.

Although compilation of the Quran was not completed for more than twenty years after the Prophet's death, he had made arrangements during his lifetime for two groups of people to protect the Quran's linguistic and compositional authenticity. The first group memorized the whole Quran and regularly recited it with the Prophet. The second group included scribes who wrote down each piece of verse or aya, i.e. the smallest part of a chapter immediately after its revelation [17]. Both groups had to agree as to the contents before the final compilation of the Quran was accepted.

According to the author, the Quranic revelations do not follow one simple style, but rather five different styles. These can be grouped according to the subject discussed in a specific verse and can be categorized as follows: (a) description of Unity or Tauhid; (b) relationship between the Creator and the creation; (c) knowledge of natural order with examples; (d) Prophet Muhammad (S:)'s life as an example to his followers; and (e) artistic and mystical narrations and simple examples from the lives of pre-Quranic messengers. (NB: These five categories exclude all discussions about law, social order, family life and detailed references to the pre-Quranic prophets, which are described in the Quran but are not relevant to this book.)

The five groups are discussed in more detail in the rest of this chapter.

(a) **Unity or Tauhid:** The style of these verses is to describe the absolute nature of God. They throw some light on how certain verses in the Quran portray the infinite nature of God but may be beyond ordinary human understanding and experience. Examples of such verses include:

'God: there is no god, but He, the Ever Living, the Ever Watchful' (2.255)
'No mortal eyes can see Him, though He sees all eyes' (6.103)
'Allah is with you wherever you may be, ever near' (57.4)
'Say: God is Unique! God is the Source (for everything) – and there is nothing Comparable unto Him'   (112.1–4)

(b) **Relationship between the Creator and creation:** The style used in these verses seems to be more comprehensible to the ordinary human mind. The verses represent commands from God and by referring to actions by man establish a bond between the Creator and the created. Examples of such verses include:

'Read in the name of your Lord Who creates,
creates man from a clot [which clings]
read, for your Lord is Most Generous,
who teaches by means of pen,
teaches man what he does not know'   (96.1–5)
'put your trust in the Ever Living'   (25.59)

Identity Through Science, Philosophy and Artistic Concepts in the Quran

'Who ordains all things' (10.32)

(c) **Knowledge:** The next style in the Quranic language explains the idea of orders, termed as laws of nature. These orders or laws are observed in creation of both the human mind and body as well as the natural universe around us. The style is direct and powerful but educational in its approach. Such explanations are helpful for those who seek to expand their knowledge. Examples of such verses include:

'this creation is in exact precision' (54.49)
'He created world and seven skies, one above another' (41.12)
'He created you in the womb of your mother – creation after creation in triple darkness'
(39.6)
'Some are alike [same] **and some are different** [not same]' (6.100)

(d) **Prophet Muhammad (S:)'s life as an example for his followers:** The fourth style shows how to apply the teachings of the Quran in practice. This comes through the implementation of social law and order by the Prophet as leader of the community. The style here is that of a speaker in a lecture room or facing an audience. Examples of such verses include:

'the Messenger of God is an excellent model –
and guides them like a shining light' (33.21)
'your only duty is to give warning, to proclaim good news' (35.22–23)
'believers, do not raise your voices above the voice of the Prophet,
nor shout aloud when speaking to him' (49.2)

(e) **Artistic:** The final Quranic style uses artistic wordings, mystical expressions and storytelling narratives that are easily understood and remain unforgettable for readers. Descriptions of the lives of pre-

Quranic messengers appear as parts of the same story but in different chapters. These verses give us an indication of the historical, social and geographical backgrounds of that time. Examples of such verses include:

'God sends water down from the sky – from the mountains come white and red marbling in different shades as well as black obsidian' (35.27, 28)
'the depths of darkness in a vast deep ocean, overwhelmed with layer topped by layer of waves, topped with dark clouds' (24.40)
'has the story of Moses reached thee?' (20.9)
'We relate the best stories to you, since We have revealed this reading to you – though before it you were heedless' (12.3)

To make it easier for us to understand the Quran's meaning, sometimes quotations from the Hadith are used. The Hadith is a compilation of the sayings and approved actions of Prophet Muhammad (S:) as he applied the Quranic revelations to his daily life. The author believes that many theological and political ideas existing in Arabia around that period would have formed the basis of his teachings. It is most likely that the Prophet applied the idea of Ijtehad in his preachings. Ijtehad means the application of knowledge based on present-day ideas in order to understand verses from the Quran.

Today we find that the Quran with its unique style has made its messenger into an internationally recognisable name. The Prophet Muhammad (S:) acted as the vehicle through which the Quran and its message of an absolute God, Creator of all space and time, could be understood. The author believes that the process would have taken the Prophet through rigorous self-recognition and increased self-awareness, making the Hadiths an additional guidance for Quranic principles to future generations.

Chapter One

BEGINNING:
ISLAM AND MEDICAL SCIENCE IN THE LIGHT OF THE QURAN

The story of human identity begins with the first Quranic revelation to Prophet Muhammad (S:) with these verses from the chapter Read:

'Read in the name of thy Lord who Createth man from a clot [which clings]; **and read thy Lord is the most Bounteous, Who teaches by the pen, teaches man which he knew not'** (96.1–5)

Man is addressed in a commanding style to understand his origin, while making the text comprehensible to the ordinary mind. In this Quranic verse the conception of the human body and development of the human mind are drawn together. The first section of this verse deals with the early development of the human form within a very limited physical boundary, whereas the next part is about the apparent limitless ability of the human mind to acquire knowledge.

Up until this revelation the concept that human beings, regardless of whether they are rich or poor, man or woman, can learn in their own right through the creative and imaginative power of the human brain had been difficult to accept. As far as the author's search has shown, this egalitarian idea did not exist in other cultures of that time and is not recorded in such an exact way in any other document or scripture from that period.

But can an individual Muslim's origin be defined today through the revelations which came in seventh-century Arabia? Many of us in the twenty-first century are under stress and strain twenty-four hours a day, seven days a week. So, how do we put into practice the Quranic philosophies that aim for a natural and holistic life for all ages? Let us begin by looking at what constitutes modern life.

In today's society life exceeds the physical boundary and enters into the domain of mental worries and anxiety, while our lifestyle is technologically advanced and complicated, most of us finding it difficult to spare much time for daily relaxation. Hence, both the body and the mind gradually becomes desperate to escape the self-obsession of society, and, failing to find an escape route, fall sick, needing a remedy. Individuals often wonder at different stages of their lives if the normal physical status that they are enjoying will last for ever.

What would happen if their health were snatched away? In the twenty-first[t] century health management includes spiritual and psychological counselling aimed at uplifting both the physical and the mental well-being of the patient. Similarly, in ancient traditional cultures such as that of the Bush people of Botswana or the Aborigines of Australia, a combination of High Spirit and remedy were used to treat sick people. These cultures combined both spiritual and physical welfare under the watchful eye and advice of the head priest in the clan, or the medicine man [18]. The main tools used for this purpose were taboos related to being clean and unclean, which determined both the spiritual and the physical well-being of individuals. In fact all religious philosophies, old and new, have expressed a healthy interest in their community's welfare.

Let us now explore Islam's attitude towards human life, which is based on the Quranic principles practised according to Prophet Muhammad's (S:) teachings.

ISLAM

Islam advocates that human life is precious and worth taking care of: **'saving life is the priority in Islam'** (6.146). It believes that the mind, body and soul are part of the natural systems of an individual. Therefore, during times of illness or stress, God wants us to preserve our natural systems through medication and prayer, as both will alleviate suffering. Hence, during illness, patience and tolerance through prayer are required, in addition to medical management, to enable the patient to fight disease, including serious illness. In Islam, Quranic teachings focus on the normal aspects of human life:

'He it is who created you and that He who maketh you laugh and weep'
(16.70; 53.43, 44)
'He is the protecting friend' (4.45; 3.150)
'[man] will be tested with good and bad times' (21.35)
'with every hardship comes ease' (94.5–8)

Humans often forget that '[man] **will be tested with good and bad times'** (21.35). The Quran advises on how to educate the restless mind and to uplift the confused state. Islamic philosophy has always encouraged the idea that the time of sickness or sorrow should be taken with the conviction that God's **'friendly protection'** (4.45; 3.150) is not far away, as God happens to be the Creator of life, so only He lets mankind pass through difficult and happy times.

This is how the Quran comforts and assures the anxious mind:

'but whoso is compelled neither craving, nor transgressing, or is forced by hunger, not by will to sin, Lo Allah is forgiving' (2,172; 5.3; 6.146)
'saving life is the priority in Islam' (6.146)

Islam advises that at times of sickness, extreme stress or when facing challenging conditions priority should be given to preserving the health and survival of the individual, as implied by: **'but whoso is compelled neither craving, nor transgressing, or is forced by hunger, not by will to sin, Lo Allah is forgiving'** (6.146). Although Muslims are forbidden to have certain types of food and drink this verse suggests that, in order to survive, an individual should try every means available to survive, even if it means eating or drinking prohibited food. So, the Quranic teachings favour saving life, rather than destroying it. The Quran teaches humans to consider life as a valuable possession: **'saving life is the priority in Islam'** (6.146).

During times of adversity we rely on support from close relatives and friends. Islam offers such support by encouraging believers to submit to God and to His commands, because '[man] **will be tested with good and bad times'** (21.35). We are encouraged to accept that God is all knowing and all sustaining and so will guide us out of adversity. In fact survival during adverse situations is one of the most important teachings in the Quran. However, mankind is also assured that hard times do not last for ever, as **'with every hardship comes ease'**(94.5–8).

Islam encompasses death as part of life, encouraging the acceptance of both life and death as part of the natural systems: **'death is a must for every living being'** (21.35). Scientific teachings confirm this basic truth for all life forms because wherever there is birth it is followed by death. Although at times humans might find that this is a difficult concept to accept we are encouraged to acknowledge death as a continuum of life.

By understanding Islam according to the Quran, mankind is directed to accept the diversity in God's natural creations as well as in the different branches of human knowledge. Conversely, the author believes that in-depth studies of these different branches of knowledge may lead us to understand and accept the One Creator and the diversity of His creations. In this chapter the aim is to explore whether there exists any relationship between Islamic ideas of the human body, mind and soul which parallel those in modern medicine.

So how does medical science describe human life in its normal condition?

MEDICAL SCIENCE

In today's medical courses, subjects like anatomy (the structural part_, physiology (the functional system) and immunology (the surveillance systems) are initially taught on the basis of the healthy human body. The study then proceeds to explain possible abnormalities that can arise owing to disorders of the natural systems. Medicine means remedy in ordinary language. This could be remedy for a physical ailment or the management of a mental disorder, or for both. Medicine also tries to eliminate the possible cause of any disease with the ultimate goal of curing the patient.

We know that medicine is generally concerned with the whole human system. Our body and mind (or psyche) together make up the complete system. The anatomical structures perform and remain in balance through genetic regulation, which takes place in the smallest cellular units of the human body. Very simply, the mental make-up of an individual takes place in the psyche, and in a healthy individual the physical and psychological conditions are well balanced. In medical terms, the development of these systems into adulthood leads to the individual's personal and intellectual identity, as well as independent actions arising from physiologically developed thought processes.

During illness, medical managements are applied according to the patient's physical and psychological need, because the ultimate aim of the clinician is to make the patient's condition as normal as possible. Some present-day clinicians try to utilise the power of the mind to lessen some chronically painful conditions [19] [20] [21]. The goal being to let the individual live a dignified and normal life.

As mentioned above, modern medicine uses advanced technological tools while maintaining a critical eye on the outcome of the treatment. However, when medical care fails to deliver the required outcome our faith in medicine and technology can be dented, and under those circumstances therapy might offer the most useful cure. It needs to be remembered, nevertheless, that unless the prognosis of therapy is beneficial for the patient and the community at large it may not be offered as a cure.

Although medicine acknowledges the terminal stage of life it aims to improve an individual's health and offer a dignified standard of living. Current advances in medical technology can be used to reverse some physiological conditions, but there are times when this is not possible and unnecessary medical intervention in such irreversible situations is not favoured by medical ethics. Modern medical management has to take into account any personal or ethical beliefs of the patient, and their family, but the outcome of such considerations may not always be medically favourable for the patient. (NB: This chapter does not aim to discuss medical management or abnormalities in any detail.)

MEDICINE IN THE QURAN

The Quran is not a theology, because it deals with the physical and mental aspects of an individual and offers them a way of life. It considers that the relationship between the body, mind and soul of an individual is their identity. The Quran teaches that this identity needs to be preserved not only in this life but thereafter. It also shows God's approval of a strong physical and moral identity in any individual. In contrast, medicine only seems to identify humans in scientific terms.

Let us now explore how the development of a human being is described in the Quran and in medical science.

THE HUMAN BODY AND THE HUMAN MIND

The Quran explains many aspects of the human anatomy that are comparable to modern biological concepts. It describes with precision some of the early developmental stages of the human body and proceeds to address the whole of mankind through a sample from the human community. The Quranic teachings address the identity of the human body, mind and soul and their relationship to the Creator. It is suggested that human identity develops from the very beginning of human conception: **'read in the name of thy Lord who Createth man from a clot** [which clings]' (96.1–5). It is revealed in the Quran that the human community exists within other natural cycles, which consist of both living and non-living systems and are part of life in this universe: **'Allah created world and seven skies and established His rules in each layer'**, **'asteroids storm over earth'**, **'God sent water down from the sky – fashioned a man from water'** (41.12) (67.5, 7) (21.30).

The Quran teaches that the true way of life is a harmonious balance from within, and is an integral part of our faith. Human identity is explained here as another creation which exists not only within a fixed period of time in this world, but also performs its normal duties through physical and mental activities.

It is important to note that in the Quran no one is described as untouchable or guilty of inherited sin; rather everybody is born equal. After birth and a finite period of stay we have to move on to the afterworld: **'man created from earth and would return to earth'** (6.95; 20.55). Traditionally, Muslims offer respect to their dead by performing a burial function as early as possible. The ceremony acknowledges the departure from this mortal world as well as the impending meeting with the Creator. The Quran does not mention or describe any other status in between this mortal phase and the immortal eternal phase.

Unlike the Bible (Lev. 13.2–7; Lev. 13, 14 15; Lev. 16.1), which describes different types of skin disorders and diseases like plague, leprosy, etc., the Quran does not discuss abnormal or pathological conditions and diseases in humans. Also unlike the Bible (Num. 19.11), the Quran does not describe death as an unclean phase. It creates a belief that death is part of human life, as whoever is born must die. It is not a sinful condition, neither is it an untouchable situation. As mentioned previously, the Quran teaches that the body is only a physical entity and that the loss of life is a universal truth. According to Muslims death is almost like passing through a hazy door from one room to another.

JOURNEY TO TRACE THE ORIGIN OF HUMAN IDENTITY

The very first Quranic revelation to Prophet Muhammad (S:) was the verse Read, which introduced fourteen hundred years ago the ideas of *conception* and *adulthood* and hence how the human identity is established. It also ascertained a connection between physical and intellectual growth in human beings. This verse is one of many such examples in the Quran, and the author believes that such references might encourage scientists today to seek further ideas mentioned in the Quran, which are only just beginning to be understood.

Different verses from the Quran and the Hadiths which can be explained through modern medicine have been discussed here under the titles of **Health** and **Remedy**.

I   **Health** focuses on:

1) Human origin (physical);
2) Human growth and maintenance;
3) Preservation of normal health, and use of nutritious items;
4) Warning against health hazards;
5) Warning against prejudice; and
6) Cleanliness.

II   **Remedy** focuses on:

1) Use of healthy food and drink in a clean environment;
2) Keeping within limits;
3) Controlling emotion; and
4) Family planning and community welfare.

I   **Health**

1) Human origin (physical)

> **'He created you in the wombs of your mothers, creation after creation in triple darkness'**   (16.78)

We know that pregnancy is a sequence of events that normally includes fertilisation or union of the sperm and ovum, followed by the implantation or attachment of the cell cluster known as a blastocyst to the uterine wall [22]. Subsequently, embryonic and foetal growth proceeds when the body starts taking shape. Medically it is now known that a human embryo grows inside three cavities which lie inside one another. The first cavity, which holds the embryo, is called the amniotic cavity. This whole structure then lies within the uterine cavity or the womb, where the development of the human embryo takes place. This is surrounded by the pelvic cavity, or the bony structure which holds the uterine structure [23]. The Quranic words '**triple darkness**' (16.78) describe this structural unit accurately.

- '**fashioned the two of a pair, the male and the female, from a small quantity when it is poured out**' (35.11; 23.13)
- '**fashioned his** [man's] **progeny from the quintessence of a despised fluid**' (75.37–9)

When the Quran says '**fashioned the two of a pair**' (35.11; 23.13) it is indicating the parental background of a human being. The woman is inseminated with the husband's seminal liquid or '**despised fluid**' (75.37–39), which has been ejected. Fertilization takes place when the discharged sperm attaches to the ovum wall and leads to the formation of an embryo or early human shape [24], i.e. the '**progeny**' (75.37–39) or a child. The family identity of an individual becomes significant at this stage according to these Quranic verses.

- '**fashioned the thing which clings** [like a leech] **into a lump of chewed flesh, and fashioned the chewed flesh into bones and clothed the bones with intact flesh – and then produced it as another creation**' (22.5)

Developmental anatomy states that the fertilized ovum (the female cell from the ovary), which is called a zygote, becomes a dense cluster of cells or blastocyst, which looks like '**chewed flesh**' (22.5) and attaches itself like a leech to the inner uterine wall, called endometrium [25]. Eventually the embryo starts branching out with rudimentary organs, and develops into three different layers, the ectoderm or outer layer, the endoderm or inner layer and another layer in between called the mesoderm. The ectoderm forms skin and nervous system, the endoderm becomes the lining of the digestive tract, e.g. stomach and intestine, whilst the middle layer or the mesoderm forms muscles and bones; in turn the bones are covered with other layers like muscles [26].

It is noticeable at this point that in the Quran the zygote is not addressed as another human but as *it*: '**produced it as another** creation' (22.5). However, we find a distinct change in the language in the next developmental stage: **'fashioned you harmoniously and in due proportion – into whatsoever form He willed'** (54.49), where the human mind is addressed as 'you' instead of 'it'.

Using the language of medicine, we know that the external anatomical positions of the body include the following aspects: front or anterior; back or posterior; and sides. If it can be imagined that there are two planes, one vertical plane (plane A) along the midline from front to back starting from the head down to the feet, and another horizontal plane (plane B) which is perpendicular to the vertical plane, both make a cross-section in the middle of the human body. This cross-section of lines anatomically divides the body harmoniously and in **'due proportion'** (54.49) into two hands, two legs, two sides of the face, etc., in the human body [27].

- 'He made you out of components' (54.49; 23.12)

Bible: Man [was created] from dust of earth (Gen. 2.7)

- 'God sent water down from the sky – fashioned a man from water' (21.30)
- 'fashioned you in stages' (84.19)

According to current wisdom, the make-up of the human body consists of several levels both structurally and functionally. The above verses indicate the lowest level of organization of a human body, which is the chemical level. It includes all chemical substances found on earth, including water, which are essential for maintaining life. The fact that water is necessary to support life [28] was included in a scripture fourteen hundred years ago, and the author believes that this point should be of importance to us.

- 'fashioned man from moulded mud' (95.4)
- 'fashioned them from sticky clay'
  (6.2; 55.14;15.26–29)

The above verses use the words **'man'** and **'them',** indicating that the insignificant clot has now reached the status where God acknowledges it as being a person. The human form is recognized here in its singular and plural identity. This also seems to be the earliest stage when God is recognising **'man'** (95.4). Additionally, the word **'fashioned'** (95.4; 6.2; 55.14; 15.26–29) can be used in medicine to describe different genetic backgrounds that contribute to human features, shapes and characteristics.

Self-recognition as an individual is then added to his or her relationship with other human beings in similar circumstances through the word **'them'** (6.2; 55.14; 15.26–29). It needs to be noted that the Quran is direct in its egalitarian approach to mankind and mentions no rank, race or gender in this natural developmental system.

We know that during implantation the cells secrete enzymes (proteins that assist chemical processes), which enables the blastocyst or cell mass to penetrate the uterine lining. During this time nourishment, which is sometimes called 'uterine milk', comes from the uterine or the inner lining wall. Eventually the blastocyst becomes oriented so that the inner cell mass is towards the inner wall. Finally, almost like the **'clay mould'** (95.4; 6.2; 55.14; 15.26–29), the human foetus is moulded from one shape to another in stages. The unidentifiable form that started its journey as a small clot now takes a form recognizable as a human being in the embryonic stage, and will eventually become a full-grown adult.

On pregnancy and the first sign of life the Hadith says 'the constituents of one of you are collected for forty days in his mother's womb in the form of a drop. Then they become a piece of clotted blood for a similar period, and then they become a lump of flesh for a similar period. Then the movement starts with spirit' [29]. Accordingly, the Hadith's idea of the human developmental period before early movement in the mother's womb can be calculated as approximately 120 days.

Medical science has verified that the first two months of development is the embryonic period. During this period the developing human is called an embryo. After the second month the development is called the foetal period, when rudimentary human organs start developing. Medically, at between sixteen to eighteen weeks of pregnancy, the foetus starts to show quick movements, a stage known as the 'quickening'

[30]. The average time between sixteen and eighteen weeks is 119 days, and indicates a parallel between the ideas in the Hadith and science.

Further sayings from the Hadith include description of a child's likeness to his or her parents, where certain characteristics come on *top* of others [31]. Genetically a child inherits characters or traits from both parents. During early embryological development the sex cells or gametes from the mother and the father choose the same characteristics through chromosomes or thread-like structures that carry genetic traits in animals or plants. For example, the characteristics for eye colour are known to group together [32]. So, if one parent has blue eyes while the other parent's eyes are brown then there is a greater probability that the dominant colour brown will be the colour of the child's eyes [33] [34]. We can theorize that the word *top* in the Hadith has been used in the same way as the medical term *dominant*.

- 'from the earth We fashioned you and unto it We shall make you return' (6.95; 32.11; 20.55)

- 'Allah multiplieth you in the earth, and unto Whom ye will be gathered' (23.79)

- 'God disposes all things in perfect order [just as He does in creation]' (27.88)

Once a human being has reached the end of his or her life, what does the Quran say about their death? The above Quranic verses give some ideas about this last phase. The earthly composition of our body was given a shape that became recognizable as a human form: **'from the earth We fashioned you'** (6.95; 32.11; 20.55). But, like any other living matter, the human body also perishes after its predetermined natural order is completed: **'unto Whom ye will be gathered'** (23.79). This process of departure, **'and unto it** [earth] **We shall make you return'** (6.95; 32.11; 20.55), from the mortal phase to the next stage takes place according to the Quran in an orderly fashion: **'disposes – in perfect order'** (27.88). It compares well with medically established knowledge.

Current medical texts describe this last human physical stage in terms of two principal changes taking place after death: contraction of muscles or rigor mortis and decomposition. After rigor mortis, the energy for chemical activity in muscle fibre is completely exhausted, and as the stiffness of the contraction passes off the decomposition, discoloration and softening of the body set in. Putrefaction leads to bacterial growth as the destruction of the body's flesh becomes prominent [35]. Finally, through different stages of **'disposal'** (27.88), the body, which is composed of a mixture of the earth's organic and mineral components, on decomposition blends with these materials, which are present in the soil.

In the above discussion on health the author has attempted to compare Quranic views with those of science about the stages that man passes through from birth to death.

2) Human Growth and Maintenance

We may ask how the Quranic philosophies would describe the human body and its growth in terms of anthropology (i.e. in its origin and social relationships).

- 'He it is who created you – from dust and a drop, then from a clot, then bringeth you forth as a child – then ye attain full strength and afterward that ye become old men – though some among you die before and that ye reach an appointed term' (16.70)

- 'Allah made you pairs. No female beareth forth save with His knowledge – no one groweth old, nor is aught lessened of his life, but it is recorded in a Book – Know that the life of this world [is] as the likeness of vegetation after rain, whereof the growth is pleasing – but afterward it drieth up' (57.20; 10.24)

We see that the Quran teaches the concept of a life cycle or a lifespan. First, a child is conceived and born; with time it grows to be a mature adult. Finally the human body shrinks with old age, when death conquers life at the **'appointed term'** (16.70). This concept of the human life cycle is in keeping with modern medical perception. Such explanations allow for a broad understanding of the components that make up our lives over time. They also signify biological and psychological events occurring with the passage of time, and are in keeping with our understanding of life today [36].

The comparison to **'vegetation after rain – it drieth up'** (57.20; 10.24) refers to the life cycle of plants as well as humans. Above all, the message is that only the Creator keeps records of all living beings and the stages of their lives. No other source can bear this responsibility.

The Quran provides further explanation of family connections and kinship, which the author believes are integral parts of human development and identity.

- **'Allah hath given you wives of your own kind, and out of them family for you – established relationship of lineage** [by men] **and kinship by women – and provided provision of good things'** (25.54)

- **'and that He who maketh you laugh and weep'** (53.43, 44)

In the above verses the Quran is reminding us of the lineage of the human nuclear family. The human growth pattern is such that it expands both vertically and horizontally. Vertically the family genealogy goes from father to son or daughter. The norm in the patriarchal family system is that the father's family name is carried forward, whilst in matriarchal cultures it is the mother's family name which continues. Horizontally, the **'family – kinship'** (25.54) extends through marriage and relationships on the mother's side.

Genetically (genes are the factors that control heredity) the male 'y' chromosome, a thread-like structure carrying male genes in animal and plant cells, establishes the father's line, whereas the mitochondrial (one of the cellular components of DNA, also known as inherited genetic characters in special proteins) establishes the mother's side [37]. In this way both the father's and the mother's attributes can be established through two different genetic strands. It is interesting to note that the Quran is guiding the human mind to think scientifically in a way that is relevant even today.

In the pre-Quranic era, the concept that both parents influenced the child's genetic traits or likeness or physical characteristics may not have been understood very well. We know that humans will generally live out their lives and use the genes inherited from their parents to adapt as necessary to their environment. For example, someone born in Alaska will have to live through extreme cold while a person born in the Sahara will experience conditions of extreme heat.

- **'Allah appointed for you the earth – and sendeth down water by measure from the sky and appointed His provision as He willeth – appointed cattle for you to ride – He is the protecting friend'** (3.150; 4.45)

The Quran also highlights the role of nature in the human struggle for survival. Rain clouds contain water molecules in exact proportion to cause rain, which pours down to soak the soil, making it ready for farming. Similarly, cattle and poultry provide food for mankind. These tell part of the human story that has helped man to establish communities and hence acquire cultural identities.

3)   Preservation of Normal Health and Use of Nutritious Items

- **'God has subjected to you** [for your use] **all things in the heavens and on the earth'** (2.168)
- **'created for them the cattle – and subdued them, so that some are for your riding, some for food – and drinks from them – good things are made lawful for you – those beasts and birds of prey which ye have trained, eat of that which they catch for you – in the cattle – drink which is in their belly, pure milk palatable to the drinker, and fruits,**

date palm, grapes, they are good nourishment – drink that cometh forth from the bee's belly [honey]where in is healing for mankind'   (16.66, 68, 69)

- 'in cattle there is drink which comes from their bellies between the bowels and the blood stream pure milk' (16.66)

- 'fish of sea is lawful for you'   (35.12)

Mankind has been a hunter-gatherer and has used agricultural methods to procure food since the beginning of its existence. Gradually man has learnt to store food for future consumption. Early on in their evolution it would have occurred to humans that certain food items brought good health, such as milk, water, etc., whilst others, such as rotten or uncooked meat, were bad for their well-being. This consciousness raised the idea of the nutritious value of food and drink as **'good nourishment'** (16.66, 68, 69). In this group of Quranic verses we see that God is encouraging the idea of healthy and nutritious foods for their effective value, and not just for taste or smell. The word **'lawful'** (35.12) applies to all good things that give good health to the individual and the community.

Examples of daily food and drink items available in Arabia in the seventh century, such as meat from hunting birds, milk from animals including cows, camels and goats, as well as a variety of fruits, are mentioned in documents from that period. Drinks like honey were naturally available, and fish was also included in the list, although there was no mention of river fish.

Scientists revealed the path of *milk circulation* in animals in detail in the late twentieth century. After food is digested in the stomach, the main nutrients from food get absorbed and carried to another part of the digestive tract by special vessels in the small intestinal walls. The nutrient is then developed through various chemical steps needed to process food and water (nutrient and water) to form milk. In ruminants, the secretion or milk is channelled from the belly or stomach and small intestines, and the liquid comes out as **'pure milk'** (16.66, 68, 69) through the milk ducts, which are not part of the capillary

Identity Through Science, Philosophy and Artistic Concepts in the Quran

channel through which it was first absorbed [38] [39]. Therefore, the Quranic description of **'from their bellies between the bowels and blood stream'** (16.66) seems to be almost identical to that in modern science.

At this point it would be appropriate to see how aptly the Quran uses the four important terms **'good – palatable – nourishing – pure'** (16.66, 68, 69), which specify and qualify the diet and nutritional habit of humans. These words signify modern ideas [40], and we come across them regularly during dietary debates. We know that to be considered of good dietary value, food has to be in good condition, be palatable, have a certain purity (not be contaminated or changed adversely) and be nutritious. It is customary nowadays to include fresh fruit as a component of our daily diet owing to its fibrous and vitamin content. Interestingly, the order of food and drink described in the Quranic list is as follows: **'meat, milk, fruit, and honey'** (16.66, 68, 69), and there is a common pattern of consumption of these items during a meal.

Historians might find it of interest to note that although the Bible mentions the use of salt in meals (Lev. 2.13) the Quran does not.

- **'Mothers shall nurse their children for two years to complete the term of nursing'** (2.233)

Nutritionally, the human milk scores high in food value, which is ideal for the growth of an infant. It has all the essential dietary components such as protein, fat, carbohydrate, minerals and vitamins. Doctors generally advise mothers to breastfeed the child as long as possible owing to the goodness of breast milk: **'nurse their children for two years'** (2.233). In the past, long-term breastfeeding was usual in most communities, as mothers had greater opportunity to look after children.

According to history, the Prophet's household practised a regime of healthy eating. Various Hadiths describe: 'Milk is both a food and a drink' [41]; 'water is a pure sweet drink' [42]; 'Prophet Muhammad (S:) loved dates, watermelon, cucumber, milk, barley bread, and meat when it was available' [43]; 'Honey, syrup of fruits, vinegar, olive oil, pumpkin, cheese etc. were in use in his household' [44]. A further Hadith advises that 'when dinner is served and the time of prayer arrives, eat first' [45], thereby giving food priority over prayer. This is probably due to the assumption that the starving mind may not be able to concentrate on prayers. It is interesting to see, as noted in an earlier example, the idea of milk as a food and as a drink, which we now know to be true because of its nutritious value [46].

4) Warning against Health hazards

'He hath forbidden you carrion, blood, swine flesh, strangled, dead through beating, dead through falling from a height, which hath been killed by horns, devoured of wild beasts – But whoso is compelled neither craving, nor transgressing, or is forced by hunger, not by will to sin, Lo Allah is forgiving' (5.4)

The Bible includes similar information about 'meat' (Lev. 7.19).

Just as today, in seventh-century Arabia dead meat or fish lying in the open for unknown periods were likely to have become contaminated by bacterial infection, bringing on putrefaction. Both these processes could arise not only from high temperatures but also from the touch of the horn, teeth, etc., of wild beasts, which could also carry bacterial infections. Similarly, science tells us that falling from a height, strangulation or beating would cause blood to collect in the injured areas, and that blood is one of the best media for accelerating any kind of infective growth. The Quranic emphasis on **'forbidden'** (5.4) can be further supported on the basis of scientific knowledge that blood and rotten tissue from dead and decomposing body parts are poisonous for human consumption because of the presence of many toxins (poisonous substances) and enzymes which are not digestible if untreated.

It is important to note that although according to the Quran certain food and drinks are prohibited under normal circumstances, God allows their consumption for the purpose of survival **'forced by hunger'** (5.4). Since adaptation in adverse situations is a natural instinct for any living species, and all branches of medicine recommend survival techniques, the author believes that this a further important parallel between medicine and the Quran.

- **'strong drink** [e.g. alcohol]**, there is some utility in it, but, the sin** [i.e. danger] **is greater than its usefulness'** (2.219)

Drinking alcohol in pregnancy is intoxicating and is not allowed in the Bible (Judg. 13.7).

In the above verse the Quran is not denying the small benefit arising from drinking, but the perceived detrimental effects of excess drink on human health overturn this. According to science, alcohol consumed in small amounts produces energy, giving us a feeling of well-being, and has been shown to be good to an extent for the circulation. But chronic long-term use of alcohol, or short-term binge drinking, or drinking during pregnancy, can have adverse effects on adult health, especially the liver, and also on foetal development. Association of alcohol abuse with liver damage was detected by the Greeks and the Indians thousands of years ago, and they concluded that chronic alcohol abuse ultimately leads to fatal conditions [47]. Today's medical literature is also full of terms like cirrhosis, cancer and other liver-damaging conditions arising from alcohol abuse.

- **'do not exceed limit in any habit'** (5.90)

A number of Hadiths also refer to excess eating and drinking: 'He [the Prophet] said avoid excess food and drink – feed the hungry – a meal for two is enough for three, and a meal for three is enough for four' [48].

Recent scientific and social advice has urged that eating and drinking habits should be kept under control, especially those of children. The UK government has issued a notice to all fast-food companies to restrict their advertisements, especially during prime-time children's television [49]. This is because current statistics show that the fat content in popular food, especially that eaten by children, is high, and is creating an obese and unhealthy society.

5) Warning against Prejudice

- **'They will ask you about menstruation, say it is impurity – leave women alone during this period'** (2.222)

Science tells us that the lining of the womb (uterus) undergoes a change each month in preparation for fertilization. If pregnancy does not occur, the lining (endometrium) is discharged as the menstrual flow [50], consisting of dead tissue and fluid. We have already discussed blood as a media for bacterial growth and infection. Traditionally people from ancient cultures have considered women during the menstrual period as *unclean*. The Bible also advocates the idea (Lev. 11.1–46, 47; Lev. 12.2–5) that the woman is not only unclean but also untouchable. On the other hand, the Quran is not asking the woman to remain in seclusion, rather specifying that this is a temporary **'period'** (2.222). It indicates that menstruation should be seen as a physical **'impurity'** (2.222) and that the woman has not committed any sin, and should not to be blamed for the bleeding. At the same time the Quran is warning men not to approach the woman for intercourse until she recovers. This is one of the earliest descriptions of God's concern for female health. It is revealed as a command to men to treat women in a dignified and considerate manner during what may be a stressful time.

- **'No blame upon the blind – nor upon the lame – nor any blame upon the sick'** (24.61)

Similar views are found in the New Testament (Matt. 18.10).

What is apparent from the above Quranic verse is God's concern that humans could become superstitious and treat others in an ignorant way which might be detrimental to their welfare. Medically it is known that although some people may be born with certain congenital conditions, other conditions, including **'blindness'** and **'lameness'** (24.61), can also arise from different causes. For example, blindness could result from eye infection due to smallpox, vitamin deficiency or even grievous bodily harm. Similarly, viral infections such as polio or severe injury could lead to a person becoming lame. Therefore, for a variety of reasons, healthy individuals may not have the use of their sight, limbs or some other bodily function, and according to the Quran no **'blame'** (24.61) should be attached to people suffering such conditions. So, human beings need to understand and respect the differences between those who are well and those who are unwell, and not treat sickness with blame or fear.

6)   Cleanliness

- **'draw not near unto prayer, when ye are drunken, till ye know that which ye utter – nor when ye are polluted —— if ye be ill – or on a journey – or cometh from the closet** [toilet] **– or have touched women** [after sex] **– clean yourself first'** (4.43)

The Quran proclaims prayer to be the highest form of all human acts and urges Muslims to feel clean and pure both physically and mentally during the act of prayer. This is apparent from the above verse. The Bible also expresses similar views regarding abstinence from the toxic effects of wine and physically unclean conditions during the time of prayer (Exod. 18.14, 15; Exod. 30.19–21; Judg. 13.14).

We know that other than physical uncleanliness, uncontrolled behaviour under the influence of some strong chemical could also make a person's company unacceptable. From a medical perspective, a person who is under the influence of any recreational drug or excess usage of alcohol may not be in control of their behaviour and may suffer from side effects such as vomiting, nausea, etc. Since a person performing his or her prayer should concentrate fully on the act, the physical action needs to be combined with an equally robust mental state, otherwise the whole concept of prayer and piety is lost.

Relevant statements from the Hadith include:

'Keep your body and mind clean – personal cleanliness is a step towards the purification of soul'   [51]
'Keep your dress and nails clean – wash hands before and after food' [52]
'Cover the milk pot and the water jar – do not breathe into the vessel' [53]

'*Miswak* [tooth cleaning with bark, a regular practice in Arabia] regularly' [54]

'Have a bath on Friday [indicating at least once a week, even in Arabia] before the congregational prayer' [55]

'Menses in women are ordained by Allah. Wash [for the women] yourself after finishing your period – and then pray' [56]

'Use salt to wash your bloodstain' [57]

The Bible (Old Testament) quite specifically mentions the cleaning of used or worn clothing and of the walls in a house; sometimes man is even asked to destroy the room used after serious illnesses, such as plague (Lev. 13.2–7; Lev. 14.35). The New Testament also counsels on cleanliness (Matt. 6.17, 18).

- **'Allah receiveth** [man's] **souls at the time of their death – and that soul which dieth not** [yet] **in its sleep – by night'** (39.42; 6.60)

The Hadith tells us that the 'eyes sleep but the heart remains awake' [58].

In the above verse the Quran points out the differences between human physiological resting and the terminal stage of death. We are aware that after death all physiological functions stop and the chemical composition of the body breaks down. It is an irreversible process. During sleep some physiological changes also take place, such as slowing down of the pulse rate, the rhythm of the heart and the respiratory rate, but these changes are reversible and the person regains normal bodily functions when he or she awakes [59].

- **'Man is painfully toiling onto God'** (84.6, 16; 90.4)

The author believes that no exploration of human identity can be complete without referring to the physical and psychological effort that man has to put into life. Physical effort may encompass a wide variety of experiences from growing pains to illnesses. On the other hand, psychological endeavour could range from dealing with the stresses of daily life to unnatural conditions such as war or famine. Both types of effort involve **'painful'** (84.6, 16; 90.4) conditions for man.

This section on Health has compared some Quranic philosophies to the precepts of modern science and shown that there exist many similarities between these apparently different subjects.

II REMEDY

The Quran, unlike the Old Testament (Lev. 13–16) or the New Testament (curing the blind and lame, Matt. 9.30; Matt. 8.3; Matt. 4.24), does not cite examples of remedy for curing diseases. In the scientific sense, a remedy is the prescription given to a sick person to cure their disease. Honey, **'drink that cometh forth from the bee's belly wherein is healing for mankind'** (16.69), seems to be the only edible item mentioned in the Quran which has been identified with healing power, although it has not been associated with any particular sick condition.

There are four main ideas that constitute the Quranic remedy for preventing sickness in general, of which three were discussed in the Health section. These were:

1. The use of healthy food and drink in a clean environment.
2. Not eating or drinking to excess.
3. Controlling emotion (under stressful conditions).

The Quranic philosophy of remedy lies in two different directions. Firstly, the Quran appeals for the use of healthy and nourishing food and drinks (natural products) to be consumed in limited amounts within a clean environment to maintain a healthy balance; secondly, the Quran asks us to remain calm in difficult situations (21.35). According to God, mankind has to face periods of hardship and ease, both as individuals and in communities (94.5–8).

In general, Muslims feel that Quranic verses have some inherent healing power. Reciting them in earnest can produce a calm and peaceful environment near a sick person, which is thought to be beneficial for their health. During such times the words 'God is with me' are believed to produce a positive effect on the patient.

On this subject the Hadith says that:

'No one should wish for death when afflicted by illness. If you cannot stop yourself, then say, 'O God, make me live as long as life is better for me, but, let me die if it is better for me that way' [60]

'Fever is from heat – leprosy is a disease' [61]

The author finds the choice of words used here interesting: *heat* for fever but *disease* for leprosy. Medically fever is not a disease but a symptom of our immune system responding to some clinical disorder. The disorder may be due to infection or a high metabolic rate, as in cancer, which produces heat. Leprosy, on the other hand, is a disease caused by a particular bacterium. Therefore the examples of a symptom and a disease are appropriately applied in this Hadith.

Other Hadiths explain that:

'Healing of some diseases can be obtained by using a potion of honey' [62]

'"Talbina" [a mixture of milk, bran and honey] was used by Aisha, the Prophet's wife, for the sick and the recently bereaved. She also advised the use of talbina-bread topped with cooked meat for the very sick. According to Aisha, the Prophet said that "talbina soothes a sick person's heartburn and helps to overcome grief"' [63].

Modern medicine acknowledges that a balanced and highly nutritious diet for patients helps to overcome illness. From the above Hadith we see that talbina contains a good mixture of protein, carbohydrate and fat from the milk component. Any good food at a time of deep shock, e.g. in bereavement, can help a person to recover by ensuring good physical health. Heartburn is usually produced in stressful conditions, in which case talbina might also be useful.

The Hadith also mentions cupping and burning of the point where a skin problem has manifested itself. But it warns that burning of the skin must be undertaken with care [64].

Identity Through Science, Philosophy and Artistic Concepts in the Quran

The author would now like to briefly discuss the medical approach or remedy theory of the Quranic age.

Medicine was practised from around the seventh century in the ancient Middle East. Historically it is said that people of that region practised a blend of three different ideas [65]:

1. Folk medicine of the Bedouins.
2. Galenic concepts (Greek ideas).
3. Prayer.

<u>Folk medicine of the Bedouins:</u> This usually employed different components of herbs, spices, water, olive oil, etc., to produce prescribed potions. Burning of some skin area (cauterization) was also used as a therapy.

<u>Galenic concept:</u> Greeks of that period used their sense of the body's humours, controlling of temperament and balancing of human characteristic as remedies. Divine invocation was sought through prayers and offerings to the superhuman spirits.

<u>Prayer:</u> The indigenous population offered prayers based on their own cultural and religious beliefs.

The Bible (the Old Testament) used isolation and special offerings by the priest as the means for making the sick regain their health (Lev. 13–15), while the New Testament (Matt. 7.7–11; Matt. 12.28) asked the sick to seek refuge in God and to believe in Jesus' healing power. The New Testament also cites examples of Jesus curing sick people such as the blind, the leper or the paralysed (Matt. 9.30; Matt. 8.3; Matt,. 4.24).

4. Family Planning and Community Welfare

The fourth type of remedy we need to explore deals with maintaining a healthy family life.

- 'good matrimonial relationship' (4.19)

According to the Quran, God has produced a harmonious balance in nature. Since a family starts with two people, a man and a woman, both need to provide time and energy for the upkeep of the family. Traditionally, the man has earned money and procured essential items for the family, whilst the woman has borne and reared children, as well as looking after her spouse and other dependent family members. According to Muslim tradition marriage is a social contract, so a balanced and harmonious relationship should exist between the married couple [66]. However, if this relationship becomes strained owing to too many extra mouths to feed and from much energy being spent on domestic chores, then it creates an unseen rift between the husband and the wife.

In order to alleviate this type of stress and hardship, and since the Quranic philosophy encourages a **'good'** (4.19) domestic environment, social medicine may be used to plan the number of children a husband and a wife wish to have. For this reason, as well as to help prevent a woman from falling ill through numerous childbirths, the author believes that family planning is essential. Additionally, the possibility of maternal death during childbirth as well as the physical hardship involved in bringing up a large family need to be addressed because **'saving life is the priority in Islam'** (6.146). The importance of the wife and mother remaining healthy and leading a normal family life needs to be respected, otherwise a close-knit community might be adversely affected.

In Islam, it is believed that Allah has asked humans to apply knowledge to establish a harmonious and rational society. If the application of medical knowledge to control the number of children results in a **'good'** (4.19) family life, then through betterment of individual(s) should come harmony in the community.

MODERN MEDICAL TECHNOLOGY AND THE MUSLIM COMMUNITY

- **'saving life is the priority in Islam'** (6.146)

How do today's Muslim communities feel about modern medical technology? Muslim communities across the world at some time face the dilemma of whether or not to use or practise certain medical procedures. In particular, treatments such as blood transfusion and organ transplantation often raise questions [67]. The author believes that since God is the creator of all knowledge, it is important to accept that science has advanced with God's help. According to the Quran **'saving life'** (6.146) is vital, and in the case of illness whatever reasonable option is available to save a patient or a community, including modern medical procedures, should be undertaken. For the author, the intention (*Niyat*) and the effort of treating a patient and the treatment itself are as important as praying for the patient.

- **'Man is chosen of God – faith is the only peace'** (25.59)

According to the above Quranic verse, prayer brings peace for both the body and the mind. Prayer can be compared to talking to God [68] and can offer mental peace [69] to the patient. Today, scientists and medical practitioners advise people not only to eat a balanced diet but also to meditate in order to reduce stress [21] [70]. To help alleviate further stress, many hospitals nowadays offer prayer facilities [71]. Immunological studies [72] [73] have shown that stress can have an effect on the body's immune system, and prayers as well as meditation can help to control stress levels.

- **'Only Allah creates from the very beginning and only He restores'** (25.59; 85.13)

However, we need to bear in mind that prayer on its own might not necessarily result in a patient being cured. A study was conducted recently on 700 heart patients who were divided into four groups. The first group received prayers according to their faith; the second group listened to soothing music, were given healing touches and imagined peaceful, beautiful places; the third group received both prayers and the healing opportunities given to the second group; and the last group received nothing. After six months the study showed no significant difference between the four groups in terms of the development of major heart problems or readmission into hospital [74]. This study shows that faith on its own does not remove an illness, **'only He restores'** (25.59; 85.13), although in the long run it may allow a person to cope better with their circumstances.

- **'sends calm and tranquillity'** (3.154)

Another study has revealed that religious faith does make one feel better: **'tranquillity'** (3.154) [75]. Although the benefits of prayer and meditation remain ambiguous, some modern health theories suggest that the practice of yoga improves the condition of the body and the soul [76]. The healers or hermits of old 'Vedic' India also used the three key words of discipline, love and grace in their approach [77] [78]. Yet another study showed that the result of meditation was improved when 'God is peace' or 'God is love' was added as a chant in meditation groups [79]. The main aim seems to be to teach the brain to relax at any time, in any place [80], and thereby help the mind to find peace.

Conclusion

It can be said that the Quranic concept of medicine, together with the Hadith's teachings, is compatible with modern life. From the Quran we are given to understand that health and remedy come not only through prayer but also by applying knowledge and effort as **'Allah loves prayer as well as deeds'** (25.29). Any attempt that results in improving the health of an individual, or the community, is desirable, whether this is in the form of medicine or prayer. The development of an individual through physical, intellectual and spiritual stages creates a sense of unique and peaceful confidence in his or her existence. Accepting the Quranic version of the beginning of the human form in a **'clot'** (96.1–5) as an individual, where **'it'** (22.5) becomes **'man'**

(21.30), and understanding and accepting the relationship of the body with the mind, can be taken as the beginning of the quest for human identity for **'them'** (6.2), i.e. the whole of mankind.

Chapter Two

LIMITATIONS: CREATION, LIFE AND ACTIVITY

In this discussion the word knowledge is used as an information tool to understand how we can interpret creation, life and activity in the light of modern science. The Quran seems to suggests that our knowledge is limited since humans have a finite ability to understand and acquire knowledge; and also live within the limitations of the mortal world: **'every matter has its appointed time'** (54.3). Although the Quranic scripture will remain unchanged we need to acknowledge that an insight of the past might help us to understand the present better [81].

As already mentioned in the previous chapter, the Prophet's role was to implement the Quranic messages by not only preaching the verses but also following them in his own life. Study of his life reveals that Prophet Muhammad (S:) put into practice the Quranic philosophies as soon as messages were revealed. He encouraged his followers to do the same. In this way faith became accessible to and accepted by the common people.

The Quran introduces its criteria for knowledge in the following way:

- 'spirit of inspiration [idea] **is the highest gift of God'** (17.5; 6.122)
- 'verify news before belief' (49.6)

We know that ideas or **'inspiration'** (17.5; 6.122) usually arise within the human mind, whereas **'news'** (49.6) is conveyed between individuals. Inspiration can arise from exceptional ideas, whereas news can relate to domestic life or the wider community. Verifying the source of the news is important for its acceptance and is a common practice in the twenty-first century. Once the source has been verified we need to then understand the news and gain any relevant information from it. To **'verify news'** (49.6) we either listen to the evidence, look at the evidence, or act out the evidence. Prophet Muhammad (S:) asked his associates to apply independent reasoning known as '*Ijtehad*' to understand earthly matters and Quranic ideas.

Professor Abdus Salam, a physicist, said in his interview with the BBC (Trieste, Italy, 1982) that 'the reason for his belief in God came from the idea of God as the fundamental source of everything'. He said that he found strength in this belief. Although belief or faith is practised by some scientists, it is not an integral part of pursuing science. In science, unless a hypothesis is examined and verified it cannot be accepted as a fact or theory [82]. Therefore scientific belief in the hypothesis requires rigorous testing and is carried out as shown in Figure 2.

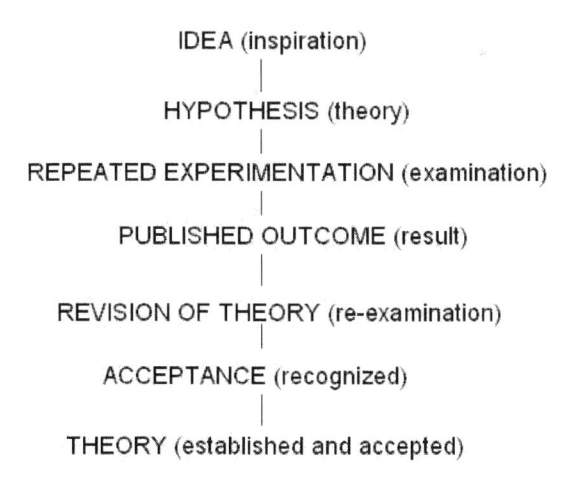

IDEA (inspiration)
|
HYPOTHESIS (theory)
|
REPEATED EXPERIMENTATION (examination)
|
PUBLISHED OUTCOME (result)
|
REVISION OF THEORY (re-examination)
|
ACCEPTANCE (recognized)
|
THEORY (established and accepted)

Figure 2. Process of scientific belief (modified from Cross, 2000, ref 82).

The flow chart in Figure 2 outlines the steps from conception to the acceptance of a scientific theory. However, the author of this article [82] also proposes that under different circumstances theories may be accepted without rigorous proof. Additionally, contemporary culture, values and beliefs also influence scientific ethics, although the philosophy of science examines only scientific methods. If the hypothesis survives repeated testing and criticisms it becomes accepted as a scientific theory. However, scientists readily admit that the laws of science are provisional and constantly evolving. The same author [83] explains that 'there are many groups of human activities which are impossible to define exactly', indicating that there may be many areas of science that are yet to be defined [84] [85]. Once a scientific theory is proven and accepted, it is then made accessible to the public. Similarly, once a Quranic verse is understood in the light of current knowledge it can be introduced to the common person. Let us now look at how Muslims have tried to assess the Quranic philosophies in the last 150 years.

Syed Ameer Ali (1839–1928) started the discussion through his book the *Spirit of Islam* in an attempt to draw the Muslim mind towards the evolution of Islam as a world religion. He stressed the importance of 'accountability of human actions' [86]. By 1930 Marmaduke Pickthall had started to inspire Indian Muslims through his lectures, which were compiled in the book the *Cultural Side of Islam* [87]. He also produced an English translation of the Quran [88]. Abdulla Yusuf Ali (1934) stirred the mass Muslim mind towards understanding their divine book with his English translation and elaborate notes on Quranic verses [89].

On the other hand, Sir Allama Muhammad Iqbal (1873–1938) tried to combine the ideas of modern Western philosophers with Quranic thoughts. He urged the modern Muslim 'to rethink the whole system of Islam without completely breaking with the past' in his book the *Reconstruction of Religious Thought in Islam*. His arguments were for understanding 'reasons behind the knowledge'. He said the main purpose of the Quran was to awaken consciousness in relation to God and the universe [90]. Similarly, at a later stage Tariq Ramadan (1999), in his book *To Be a European Muslim* [91], tried to relate the issues facing Muslims living under the influence of Western civilization.

The question today is whether time is a barrier for understanding the Quranic philosophy, especially if it is expressed in modern terms. It is reasonable to assume that the knowledge gained and the activities performed by an individual during any period in history will shape their character and identity. It is accepted that the knowledge and the activities of any generation are not only relevant to that generation, but build up a picture for future generations about how that period might be represented in history. For example, Genghis Khan and Albert Einstein are remembered in history as a conqueror and a famous physicist, respectively. The activity or knowledge pursued by each defined their individual inspiration and identity, which still stands irrespective of time. While both followed their natural inspiration and philosophy, their efforts were ultimately limited through death, i.e. each had an **'appointed time'** (54.3).

HUMAN KNOWLEDGE FROM THE QURAN

In other words knowledge can be interpreted as information. In Islam it is believed that all living species, whether human, animal, bird or insect, have an inherent knowledge base that enables their species to survive. It can be said that Nature or God's creative process does not stop but is endlessly moving forward. This wealth of information that is continuously growing has to be discovered and understood by man. The process of implementing knowledge and then advancing on that basis is probably unique to humans.

There are many verses in the Quran which stress the importance of human knowledge. Only a handful of these verses have been selected for our purpose. These verses can be grouped into three different categories:

1. The Definition of Knowledge.
2. How Knowledge is Acquired.
3. The Benefits of Knowledge.

The Definition of Knowledge

'God is the Light, Knowledge and Truth'   (24.35)

'in this Book there are examples for people of understanding'
(51.20) '[there are] **signs** [examples] **from God for the understanding mind'** (3.190)
'Allah leads human mind from darkness to light' (57.9)
'verify news before belief' (49.6)

These verses describe knowledge according to the Quran. The message here is that if we do not acquire knowledge then we will remain ignorant and in **'darkness'** (57.9). The author believes that since **'God is the Light, Knowledge and Truth'** (24.35), to understand knowledge is to comprehend God and creation. Also, knowledge is **'for the understanding mind'** (3.190) that pursues truth with determined perseverance. However, as mentioned earlier, we need to **'verify news before belief'** (49.6). Just repeating or copying the information without understanding is not sufficient. God wants critical judgement because only when the human mind has understood and accepted a piece of information can it become useful. Similarly, the Quranic messages can be established and recorded [92] only after they have been critically scrutinized. Ignorant minds can misunderstand the truthful philosophy behind Quranic teachings and take refuge in biased superstition, which is strictly prohibited in the Quran: **'it was not God who instituted** [superstition]**'** (5.106; 6.144).

In sura Ya-Sin we find that:

'Allah intended to give man his limited free will or power of choice [limited freedom of thought and activity]. **So, with sight and power of motion, man can notice and can save himself from the wrong** [accustomed path]. **Had it not been God's will, man would have rushed headlong upon their wonted path** [and would be doomed forever from not taking the right decisions]' (36.58–68)

The above verse explains the power that has been given by God to humans. We are allowed to think and act with choice within a **'limited free will'** (36.58–68). The ability to choose the right or wrong act, thought or inspiration will eventually increase man's knowledge and understanding of his surroundings, which in turn become part of his

Identity Through Science, Philosophy and Artistic Concepts in the Quran

character and identity. When humans use their limited **'power'**, in this case their knowledge and the resulting actions (e.g. a fisherman knows how to catch fish), they **'act with choice'** (36.58–68).

The above excerpts from sura Ya-sin also hint at the human tendency to choose the wrong or **'wonted path'** (36.58–68). Since humans can distinguish right from wrong, whereas animals may behave *wrongly* as part of their survival instinct (e.g. a dominant male wolf will fight to gain territory), we have a higher status in the evolutionary hierarchy. This is an important step in mankind's developmental history and has been highlighted in the Quran. Man also has the ability to plan for the future and act accordingly (e.g. plan to buy a car and save money towards it) – a trait which may not be found in all species. Importantly, despite man's limited knowledge and his ability to be **'wrong'** (36.58–68), humans can dominate humans and other species. Therefore, knowledge allows us to make informed decisions and helps us to shape our identity.

The author believes that through the above verses the Quran is establishing humans' ability to choose, while pointing out that such choices are restricted. In other words, while the power to choose is important and in many ways defines our life experiences as well as the knowledge we acquire, we need to practise this **'free will'** (36.58–68) with restraint.

How Knowledge is Acquired

'the Quran, recite and contemplate'	(3.191)
'God speaks through inspiration'	(42.51, 52)
'knowledge is taught through inspiration'	(6.106)
'everything is recorded things visible and not visible'	(54.53)
'knowledge of created natural systems which are not known'	(16.8)
'man gets knowledge through pen and record'	(68.1)

The above group of verses relate to how knowledge is acquired. The first option suggested is through the deliberation of existing knowledge, i.e. to **'contemplate'** (3.191), while a second option would be through **'inspiration'** (42.51, 52) (6.106). Now learning arises through perseverance and the exploration of ideas almost in the same way as science accepts or rejects 'hypotheses' on the basis of repeated experimentation [93]. According to science, knowledge is gained when the conscious mind translates an inspiration or idea into a series of thoughts [94], and through repeated testing gradually provides an insight into a hypothesis. Such a trial-and-error process might also bring forth new facts and information. It would be sensible to suggest that despite such a rigorous process any knowledge that still remains beyond our understanding would be the **'unknown'** [95] [96] [97].

When the Quran says with **'pen and record'** (68.1) man achieves knowledge, it means that there is no short cut, and only with much hard labour can the searching and understanding mind attain knowledge of the **'natural systems which are not known'** (16.8). As mentioned earlier, this is comparable to the scientific approach of accepting a hypothesis through repeated experimentation [98]. In simple words, by writing down ideas and **'recording'** (68.1) the outcome man creates knowledge which then becomes part of a larger philosophy. In the same way, the word **'pen'** (68.1) could have been used in a symbolic way in the Quran to indicate that knowledge could exist in a written form, while the word **'read'** (96.1–5) encouraged Muslims to seek knowledge across the horizon: **'recorded things visible and not visible'** (54.53).

The above verses make it clear that knowledge is to be acquired for achievement and application, and tested for its validity.

The Benefits of Knowledge

'knowledge is beneficial, it is from Allah' (2.269; 3.190; 31.34)
'man's superiority over others is through knowledge' (70.39)
'intellect or power of knowledge overcomes objection'
(61.8; 84.19)
'true light of knowledge comes through revelation' (64.8)
'increase knowledge [with piety]**'** (20.114)

The Bible also mentions the 'Tree of Knowledge' (Gen. 2.9).

This group of verses indicates some of the **'beneficial'** (2.269; 3.190; 31.34) effects of knowledge on both the individual and the society. However, knowledge may also bring a sense of power or **'superiority'** to man, which may be used to dominate **'other'** humans or living creatures (70.39). Science has helped man to gain technical advancements and thereby to influence both living and non-living systems. The author believes that the real benefit of knowledge comes not only from advancing the scientific frontiers but from using them in ways which are beneficial to society. Otherwise, knowledge which is not of benefit to man might ultimately bring about his downfall. The author also holds piety in high regard and feels that knowledge should be gained through piety and respect for God. History tells us that Muslims have overcome obstacles and pioneered many fields of knowledge (e.g. algebra, engineering, astronomy, medicine) [99] [100] through their belief in **'increas**[ing] **knowledge** [with piety]' (20.114).

Knowledge can be used to establish human identity when we use our power of choice wisely, rather than misusing it, which eventually leads to the fall of society. The next section on creation, life and activity attempts to clarify how the pursuit of knowledge may be damaging to mankind.

CREATION

Verses grouped under this heading are subdivided into sections for easy understanding. The aim is to understand our surroundings, which comprise and contribute to the living world, through the Quran.

1.

'Allah is the sole Creator of all being'	(59.24)
'all are governed by His law under His command'	(75.4)
'only Allah creates from the very beginning and only He restores it'	(85.13)

This collected group of verses gives insight into the source of creation. They indicate that God, the Creator, has established the whole of creation according to a precise scheme. Since science similarly tells us that natural laws govern the universe, there seems to be a parallel with Quranic philosophies.

Although the Quran maintains that only God **'creates – restores'** (85.13) and re-creates nature, science has not yet accepted the idea of a single original source of creation. But as discussed earlier in this book [83], scientists readily admit that the laws of science are provisional and constantly evolving, and that 'there are many groups of human activities that are impossible to define exactly'. So it is possible that one day God or the Creator of the natural worlds might be fully understood by science.

2.
'"Be" [or] "Kun" happened in a very short period' (54.50; 6.73)
'sky and the universe were blended into a smoky pulp.
They were separated' (26.30; 41.11)
'God alone holds the key of knowledge and time within a space' (30.8; 58.7)
'the created universe is governed by laws' (54.53)
'each large and small particle [matter] **– is recorded'** (10.61; 50.3–4)
'God alone is aware of all records' (54.53)
'Allah's rule [or] command does not change' (30.30)
'Allah created other unknown things'
(10.20; 16.8, 12; 77; 31.20; 27.75; 72.26)
'travel through the earth and see how God originated creation' (29.19)
'contemplate the wonders of creation' (3.191)
'recite and contemplate the Quran, practise and implement the principle' (17.45–48)

The Bible (Gen. 1.3) also expresses similar ideas on God's absolute power in creation.

To understand the Quranic verses one needs to **'contemplate'** (3.191) its meanings. Unlike the Bible, the Quran does not indicate

Identity Through Science, Philosophy and Artistic Concepts in the Quran

that creation started with the word 'Light', but rather with 'Be', which is a command from God. It signified the beginning of an explosive event. This explosion is thought to have created a **'time within a space'** (30.8; 58.7) as the **'sky and the universe were blended into a smoky pulp – they were separated'** (26.30; 41.11) [101] [102].

In modern science the Creation of matter is believed to have started through an explosion called the Big Bang. So perhaps the word **'Be'** (54.50; 6.73) from the Quran can be taken as a comparable term for Big Bang. According to quantum cosmologists, Big Bang created 'time' from 'space' in a very rapid and continuous manner. Immediately after this spectacular phenomenon, ripples from this explosion were carried to its boundaries. The Cambridge space telescope traced one such image of ripples in the cosmos [103] [104] [105] [106] [107]. In the Quran, God declares the creation of **'time within a space'** (30.8; 58.7), so according to the Quran the 'reality' of time became apparent only when there was 'space'. The Quran also implies that knowledge of that creation is also with Him, but He does not give a reason for this creation.

Everything that is created is made up of matter. Matter includes the air we breathe, the water we drink and all living and non-living objects. Atoms were thought to be the smallest unit of matter, although science has more recently described the existence of subatomic matter. A reference to this has been made in the Quran in terms of **'each large and small particle** [matter]' (10.61; 50.3–4). Astronomy, physics, chemistry, biology and other branches of science have continued to study the properties of matter, and scientific methods have confirmed that there are **'laws in nature'** (54.53). These natural laws govern all particles of matter, irrespective of its size, shape or status. Nature's laws started at the beginning of time, and are repeated in continuous cycles, except under abnormal conditions. The Quran indicates that there is no end to the creativity in nature; it is a continuous process holding many **'unknown things'** (10.20; 16.8,1 2; 77; 31.20; 27.75; 72.26). In fact God seems to be urging man to explore the **'wonders of creation'** (3.191).

However, we know from science that the laws which govern earth and the universe are precise and do not break down easily. Although all natural processes are repeated again and again through these laws, some processes still remain unknown to man. Time is the only factor that seems to change during such repetitions.

These Quranic verses draw our attention to that point in time when all ideas, matters and the movement of time began. Time helps the acquisition of knowledge to progress, and is constrained only by human limitations.

3.
'lofty sky, spreading universe – there are measuring units in this which should not be overlooked'	(55.7–8)
'Allah created world and seven skies. He established His commands	
[and] **rules in each layer'**	(41.12)
'each layer of this sky is created'	(65.12; 71.15)
'spreading sky and stars that recede'	(81.15; Y. Ali)
'moving night'	(89.4)
'asteroids storm over earth'	(67.5, 7
'This creation is in exact precision'	(54.49; 67.3)
'creation is in due proportion'	(82.7)
'natural laws do not change'	(30.30)
'only Allah creates and holds all records, – some known, some not known'	(72.26; 77)
'some are the same and some are different'	(6.99, 100)

The Bible: 'God and His strength in creation – in skies, rain and wind' (Jer 51.15–18).

Again we come across Quranic verses covering natural laws that regulate the infinite varieties in the creative process. What does the verse **'each layer of this sky is created'** (65.12; 71.15) mean? Now, we can describe anything that we see when we look up as *the sky*. Using modern scientific technology we have been able to photograph certain parts of the sky and our surrounding atmosphere. These photographs are computerized images which show that earth's atmosphere has several layers starting from the earth's surface upwards. These are: the *troposphere*, which contains the breathing air; the *stratosphere*, which contains the ozone layer; the *mesosphere*; the *thermosphere* and the *exosphere*, which make up the middle layers; the sixth layer is called the *magnetosphere*; beyond this remains the seventh layer of the sky, which can be called 'space' [108].

Identity Through Science, Philosophy and Artistic Concepts in the Quran

Science tells us that there is proof, as the Quran states, of **'stars that recede'** (81.15; Y. Ali). In N. J. Dawood's *The Koran*, the translation points to **'a star which rises and sets'** (81.15). But how is the direction of a star determined, i.e. if it is setting or rising? A series of photographs taken by the Hubble space camera suggest that stars, like any other created matter, change from their beginning, i.e. at birth when they are a new star, to the end, when they reach their gaseous state, with each stage showing a different colour [109]. These differences in colours, as well as changes in brightness, are taken as the capacity of the star's gaseous power. The use of hydrogen enables the star to shine, but when hydrogen becomes low the light of the star dims. Hence the **'receding – or setting'** (81.15) of stars as stated in the Quran may be referring to their fading light.

The Quranic idea of **'moving night'** (89.4) seems appropriate for describing sunlight and the path taken by light. As we know, daylight or the sun's rays fall on those areas which face the sun; while darkness covers the land as soon as sunlight moves away. This happens repeatedly as the earth orbits around the sun. We know from astronauts that in space everything seems to float in a dim light in between daylight and pitch dark. Therefore the night moving across the earth can be visible from space, showing that part of the earth's surface where the sun's rays are not shining.

Science also tells us that asteroids or rocks travel in fixed paths or orbits in space. Asteroids, meteorites and so forth sometimes enter the earth's atmosphere [110] [111], which result in areas being showered with asteroids, or **'asteroids storm over earth'** (67.5, 7).

Both the Quran and scientific endeavours remind us again and again of the simple rule that **'this creation is in exact precision – natural law does not change'** (54.49; 67.3; 30.30). Nature always follows the same precise principle, be it in the composition and replication of life's signature molecule, DNA [112], or a water molecule, which is always composed of two parts hydrogen and one part oxygen. Repetition of such natural processes allows proliferation or growth throughout the universe.

The author believes that mention of the process of deviation in nature is now necessary. This idea of deviation from the normal may be associated with the Quranic verse **'only Allah creates and holds**

all records – some known, some not known' (72.26; 77), indicating that the record can change and may be known only to Allah. Therefore the important point is that natural laws are precise in replication and within limitation, although deviation from the known can also occur – for example, a mutation which results in the evolution of an organism, i.e. **'some are the same and some are different'** (6.99, 100).

4.

'moon's route, sun's route and their appointed time – stars also'
(21.83; 36.38–40)
'sun's route and its moving contents' (36.38)
'shadow and its length, relationship with sun' (25.45, 46)

The Bible expresses the same idea to an extent (Gen. 1.16, 19).

This group of Quranic verses refers to the celestial bodies that are part of our solar system. All celestial bodies follow their own routes. The sun, moon and stars all rotate routinely in their own orbits. On earth anything which comes between the sun and the earth will cast a shadow. Also, the shadow of the obstructing object becomes shorter or longer depending upon the time of the day. If the sun's rays fall directly on the object, say on a tree at midday, then its shadow is shortest in size. Similarly, the shadow of the tree will be longer when the light falls at an angle. This phenomenon compares well with the Quran's description of **'shadow and its length, relationship with sun'** (25.45, 46).

5.

'mountains and its firmaments are in proper balance – and rivers, roads and land marks – that you may be rightly guided' (78.7)
'the process of creation is repeated' (29.19)

This group of Quranic verses conveys ideas on our natural environment. Mountains are seen as solid structures that are immobile, fixed firmly on the surface of the earth. The firm positioning of the mountains, rooted inside the earth's surface, could be compared with pegs or dowels that fit into holes and join together two adjacent parts in the soil [113]. Like all creative processes, the process of mountain roots or bases penetrating the crust of the earth has been **'repeated'** (29.19) throughout history. The layout of **'mountains'** (78.7) serves another purpose as humans, and perhaps even animals, learn to use these mountains as **'land marks'** (78.7). Similarly, **'rivers'** which flow through fields, between mountains and around forests also play an important part within the habitat of the local area, including providing sustenance and **'land marks'** to humans and animals (78.7).

6.

'vacuum [air] is easily circulating' (51.1–3)

The clue given to us in this verse is about something that moves and yet is not visible. The term 'circulating' can be applied only when something moves as a living body, or within a living body (like blood), or to matters such as a gas or fluid, which move within a space or atmosphere. Although the above Quranic verse uses the term **'vacuum'**, air may be the most appropriate term to describe it. Therefore this verse can be interpreted with modern scientific knowledge as referring to the atmospheric belt that contains essential components of life, such as oxygen, carbon dioxide, nitrogen and hydrogen, which are **'circulating'** (51.1–3) around the earth's surface [114].

According to science, the part of the atmosphere which is essential for life is the biosphere, which is responsible for creating habitats for living organisms [115]. Different habitats, which have come into being in different parts of the world, have their own characteristics to support a variety of living creatures. The ecosystem of each habitat is influenced by a variety of factors present within the biosphere, including water content, temperature and gaseous matter [116]. These essential components circulate within the atmosphere of the habitat and are important for keeping organisms alive. They maintain a balance between life and death as well as between growing and sedentary populations – processes which are integral to the natural cycles that sustain our ecosystem.

So we can understand from science how important it is that **'vacuum [air] is easily circulating'** (51.1–3) around us.

7.

'time in periods [small, medium and long] – **a definite period has been allocated for each creation'** (54.3)
'all created matters are in two phases' (6.73)
'every matter has its appointed time' (54.3)

The Bible echoes the same idea (Gen. 1.26–28, 31).

Here the Quran covers a subject that is largely unknown to us. It is difficult for us to fathom how time has been allocated by nature as separate functional periods for different living and non-living systems. Time is usually mentioned in the context of a defined unit – for example, seven days have been allocated for a week, and twelve months for a year. The Quran, however, has different views about the use of **'time periods'** as units (41.9, 12; 41.10; 7.54; 32.4; 18.19; 32.5; 70.4).

Some examples of this are:

- ❖ **Creation in 2 days**
- ❖ **Creation in 4 days**
- ❖ **Creation in 6 days**
- ❖ **One day or part of a day**
- ❖ **One thousand earthly years**
- ❖ **Fifty thousand earthly years**

Perhaps these Quranic verses are referring to time in terms of daily units as well as other units such as light years. They could be denoting time as the minutes or days or years taken for a particular organism to mature – for example, for a plant seed to mature into a tree or a virus to multiply. What we currently understand is that time flows forward from one event to another, whereas space remains still [117], and perhaps at a future date we will understand the significance of the above references to **'earthly years'**.

The Quranic view that each living or non-living system has its **'appointed time'** (54.3) is relevant, because the concept of finite existence is within our space–time perception of life. The Quran also points out that **'all created matters are in two phases'** (6.73), i.e. that both living and non-living matter have a temporary existence in this life and that nothing is immortal. Additionally, this verse could be interpreted as a reminder to all living creatures that they have to pass through the two stages of birth and death, separated only by a limited existence on this planet.

8.
'the [last] day everything will be destroyed – "big crash"'
(82.1–3; 84.1–4)
'unknown collision [star or comet] **– terrible vibration – unimaginable sound – blazing fire – when the earth shall quiver – mountains crumble into heaps of shifting sand'**
(69.13)
'God disposes all things in perfect order [just as He does in creation]' (27.88)
'all created matters are in two phases' (6.73)

This group of verses reflects on the final stage of creation. They refer to the end of the appointed term after which all matter will be disposed of, since the **'two phases'** (6.73) of the creative process include destruction. It is noticeable that except for the **'big crash'** (82.1–3; 84.1–4) no other natural destructive phenomenon has been described in the Quranic verses.

Scientific studies depict the Big Bang as a phenomenon from the past [118]. These studies also presume that there is a possibility of a 'big crunch' in the future [119]. Scientists believe that the universe has been expanding since its birth, **'spreading sky and stars that recede'** (81.15; Y.Ali), and suggest that the universe is expanding at such a rate that one day there may be a 'big crunch' or a **'big crash'** (82.1–3; 84.1–4). According to scientists, at the time of such an event **'terrible vibration – blazing fire – crumbling of lofty mountains to sandy dust'** (69.13) might occur.

The Quran also notes that the disposal of any matter follows a pattern, i.e. the **'process of disposal is always in perfect order'** (27.88). Some supporting examples of this Quranic view would be:

1) if somebody is affected by 'flu' or 'malaria', the disease or the destructive process would behave in the same way whether the person comes from Canada or from the Sahara desert;
2) the destructive steps of deforestation, desertification, etc., would follow the same path whether in Indonesia or in Brazil;
3) when earthquakes, floods, tsunamis or other natural disasters occur, the process of destruction is the same anywhere in the world whether it be in India or the USA.

This concept of an orderly disposal seems to follow on from the Quranic philosophy of **'two phases'** (6.73), i.e. the creative and destructive processes faced by all living and non-living matters (also see 'death' in Chapter 1).

So far the discussion on creation has shown how the Quran has revealed ideas or knowledge of the creation and destruction of the universe. These ideas can also be explained in the light of contemporary scientific knowledge. All Quranic and scientific ideas on the surroundings of our living world or the biosphere point towards the fact that there is a beginning and an end of all matter through space and time.

LIFE, A SPECIAL CREATION

'Man's first creation from "no existence" to this life and then "existence after death"' (45.13; 76.1)

Allama Iqbal, the poet, discovered a unique way of looking at man's life through the above verse from the Quran. It is important to mention that, in terms of this section, the word life embraces both human and other living beings. But when it comes to knowledge, activity and an afterlife, it refers to mankind only. We know that knowledge qualifies and strengthens the life of a person or a community. There are various expressions of life and the living in the Quran, such as its natural habitat or living processes, its good or bad actions; this implies that there is a formula for life that possibly fits every living being.

For humans this formula is the 'Mortal Formula of Life' (Figure 3), where (A) will lead to (B) which will lead to (C) and finally to (D). According to the Quran all living beings follow this routine. Each life is born (A) as a single being from its ancestor or progenitor; thereby initiating the process of life and growth (B); propagation or continuation and maturation is the next phase of extension (C); which stops with death or demise of the life form (D). In this way the mortal cycle of life continues from birth to death, and celebrates the life's existence within a limited period. Here it is noticeable that the basic requirements and continuity of one life, be it human or otherwise, do not vary much from another. **'Man's first creation from "no existence" to this life and then "existence after death"'** (45.13; 76.1) summarizes the 'Mortal Formula of Life'.

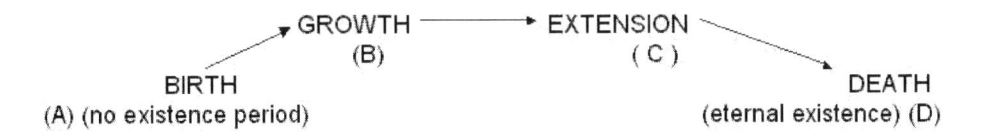

```
              GROWTH  ———→  EXTENSION
                (B)              (C)
         ↗                            ↘
    BIRTH                               DEATH
(A) (no existence period)         (eternal existence) (D)
```

Figure 3. The Mortal cycle of human life

The following Quranic verses represent the creation and qualify the meaning of life. They have been arranged in several sequential groups:

1.
'earth is a habitable place'   (21.30; 77.25)

This verse states that life in its current form is suitable for this planet because all essential requirements, such as temperature, moisture and the atmosphere, are ideal to sustain life. According to current scientific literature, even if all chemical elements required for the soup of life combined in the most ideal atmosphere or conditions, something else would still be needed to start the *spirit* of life. Based on our current knowledge, it would be difficult for man to re-create the **'earth's habitat'** (21.30; 77.25) and the primordial soup or life's first letters to assemble the chemical molecules of a living being [120] [121] [122].

2.
'He kindles the light of dawn' (57.9; 113.1)
'He has ordained the night for rest' (25.47)

The Quran leads us to believe that God commands and controls the cycle of life, including the beginning and the end of day and night. Science has established that both physically and psychologically human life is dependent on sunlight. Additionally all living beings, except nocturnal creatures, require sunlight, and for most creatures night is the time for rest. Even DNA, the molecule of life, has a resting phase. So the implication in the above verses seems to be that all living beings follow nature's rule of work and rest. **'The light of dawn'** (57.9; 113.1) may also refer to the beginning of life as originating from God.

3.
'spiders cobweb – as dwelling' (29.41)
'it was He who created you from a single being and furnished you with [a dwelling and] **a resting place'** (6.98; 4.1; 39.6; 69.13)

In these verses the word **'dwelling'** refers to a place of residence. Communities or an individual will usually choose a place of dwelling or living that is suitable to start and nurture life. This is especially true for creatures of higher life form, e.g. humans or apes. In many human communities, the place of dwelling is where life is continued from previous generations and becomes the living place for future generations. On the other hand, **'resting place'** (6.98; 4.1; 39.6; 69.13) is usually a place needed for sleeping. For example, a person can come back from work or travel to a place to rest. It may or may not become his permanent dwelling place. Similarly in nature we have seen how migratory birds use selected sites as their resting place before continuing on their journey.

4.

'water is the source of life'	(24.45)
'it is He who sends down rain from sky – buds of every plant – behold when their fruits ripen'	(80.26–31)
'Allah creates seed – embryo – plant or tree'	(6.95)
'it is God Who splits the seed and the fruit stone'	(80.26–31)

The Bible informs us that the tree of knowledge contains both 'good' and 'bad' knowledge (Gen. 2.9).

Many years ago scientists proved that **'water is the source of life'** (24.45) [123]. Although water alone cannot create life, and requires other key components, it is universally accepted that humans cannot exist without water. In fact, scarcity of this precious item can lead to death.

The above Quranic verses suggest how water in the shape of rain helps life to grow. We know that various life cycles exist in nature, and the references made here are for vegetation. It is explained that a **'bud'** (80.26–31) becomes a flower, which in turn becomes a fruit. Fruits then produce seeds, which develop into the next stage of maturity, an **'embryo'** (6.95). The embryo or seed in turn then grows or germinates under favourable conditions to form a plant and eventually a mature fruit-bearing tree. Subsequently, God splits the **'seed and the fruit stone'** (80.26–31) and allows the whole phenomenon to start again. This process is a part of the natural biological cycles that encompass the natural world.

It is implied in the Quran that this kind of growth, where seeds, embryos, fruits and plants all follow God's natural order, arises from good knowledge. Whereas man's growth of knowledge, when specifically applied to self or only for profiteering, can be bad knowledge; especially if it unbalances the natural order and the ecosystem.

5.
'each life has been numbered separately' (19.94)
'the process of creation is repeated' (29.19)

The Quran asserts above that **'each life'** has been allocated a specific term. Scientific interference may change some natural orders, but ultimately it does not influence the overall time span of life by much. The Quran specifies that each individual being is created **'separately'** (19.94) and that the record book of nature does not forget anything. Therefore the order of life will be carried out and **'repeated'** (29.19) in due time in a perfect manner.

6.
'man created from earth and would return to earth' (6.95; 20.55)
'life [all so far known] **is starting from earth and back to earth'** (23.79)

According to these Quranic verses **'earth'** is where life exists and man and all living beings need its planetary environment to survive. The full cycle of life, for known life forms, starting from birth and ending in death, occurs on this planet. Common sense dictates that man's individuality starts with life at birth, and goes hand in hand with the culture and customs of the birthplace. The above verse, **'life starts from the earth'**, means it starts with earth as the baseline, whereas the factors discussed in the previous sections encompass life. Death brings man **'back to earth'** (23.79) and we are left with only the earthly remains in the dust [124] resulting from the chemical decomposition of the body (see also 'death' in Chapter 1).

7.

'the likeness of the present life is like rain'	(10.24)
'death is a must for every living being'	(21.35)
'destiny of life goes as part of the natural cycle'	(39.68; 28.88)

An integral part of our life is **'rain'** (10.24). When it falls it creates a beautiful atmosphere, especially in arid places such as the Arabian Peninsula, where after rainfall green vegetation flourishes for a while, bringing new colour and a fresh smell. Soon after water from the rain recedes and the sun's heat begins to rise, the new vegetation (following a period of initial growth) will shrivel up and die. This is a good simile for **'life'** (10.24) – when life is new it is young and fresh, but eventually it reaches the end of its life cycle and becomes old and dry before **'death'** (21.35).

The discourse so far on life's meaning, or our understanding of what is meant by life, shows our dependence on how life is sustained in the living environment. No life can continue without this support, although **'destiny of life goes as part of the natural cycle'** (39.68; 28.88). However, despite excellent advances in science it does not tell us why life started. What the ultimate key that switched on life on this planet was has yet to be identified, and the only point that is certain is that life started and is not immortal.

HUMAN HABITAT AND ACTIVITY

A definition of habitat or natural environment has already been given in a previous section. We know that although some species inherit the same habitat, which then needs to be shared out according to the needs of the species, many living beings find that their ideal living place is not suitable for others. The ability to adapt to a variety of living conditions seems to be relatively simpler for human communities than it is for plants, animals and other living beings. In such non-human societies habitat plays a major role in establishing identity.

In contrast, human identity builds on or comes from the habitat as well as the actions of individuals, amongst other factors. Human or animal identity develops from the surroundings or the community in which he or she grows up. Their personality or character is also influenced by their experiences of life. The perception of 'I' or 'Me' as self is an important foundation of the human identity, and is in fact recognized as such by a special area within the human brain. This area supports the concept of self or the identity of an individual human being.

On a wider note, an individual's identity when combined collectively with those of other relevant individuals will produce the identity of a community. A community is usually referred to as a group of individuals living in a place with similar culture, scope and facilities, and often with similar general interests. Under these circumstances, the occupation of an individual thereby becomes an important factor or condition of their identity. For example, a poet, a farmer or an engineer all contribute in different ways to the community while enjoying the benefits offered by the collective identity of that population. The author believes that a major part of the identity of a human being also comes from their actions, i.e. the actions performed describe a person's character.

We need to remember that all human communities share the biosphere (air, light and water) with other non-human life forms. According to scientists, habitat initiates different kinds of activities in different animals and, along with characteristics such as size, shape and colour, defines the animal's identity. Therefore, the ecosystem in which animals live contributes towards their identity. This includes: the areas where they may be found, what kind of food they eat, their relationship with that particular environment, where their offspring are brought up, as well as their ability to cohabit with humans.

In this section the Quranic examples on habitat and the actions of mankind will be discussed separately. The following discussion will be based on the habitat and activities which are integral to human identity.

HABITAT

'earth is a habitable place'   (21.30)

The habitat for living beings including humans is described in the Quran in the context of the Arabian Peninsula. The idea is to form a relationship between life forms and their surroundings in a way which could be recognized in the seventh century. The Quran also narrates some activity and interrelationship between humans and the lives of relevant neighbouring communities.

'valley of the ants'	(27.18–19)
'pasturage on which cattle feed'	(80.24–32)
'contemplate on camels – how they were created – the mountains – raised high – the earth – made flat'	(88.17–20)
'birds can fly and float – God sustains them'	(67.19)
'bees have home – hives – in mountain and trees'	(16.68)
'quails in desert'	(20.81)
'spiders cobweb – as dwelling'	(29.41)
'ocean and its fresh fish'	(16.14)
'valley of sand dunes wind craft sand hills'	(46.21)
'this book is given in your own language'	(13.37)
'Arabs of the desert'	(9.97)

The Bible: 'Stork in the sky knows her season, the turtle, dove, swift and crane keep the time of their coming' (Jer. 8.7).

These verses throw light on the habitat of each living being, such as its dwelling place, its nature, the resources for its food and how it was involved with the desert-dwelling Arabs. They create a picture of the ecosphere, or living area, where man, animals and insects interact in the desert. Arab people (especially from the Hijaj area) were well acquainted with ants from the valley; they grazed their cattle in green pasture, and their camels came from the mountains and flat fields around these mountains. The Arabs must have seen birds flying in the air and probably wondered how they remained afloat. They used honey from beehives that came from the trees in nearby mountains. They used quail for meat while fish was caught only in the sea, and not rivers. Spiders are described as spinning their cobwebs for dwelling purposes.

Biology, geography, geology, ecology and other scientific disciplines explore similar ideas in that they too are studying how creatures in the natural world coexist in perfect balance and harmony.

It is interesting that the Bible's description of the human habitat is different from the Quran's references to desert life. In the Bible storks and other birds of that group, which are not a familiar sight in the Arab desert, are mentioned. This indicates that the Bible's background is probably a place where water was not a scarce resource.

ACTIVITIES

The author believes that the Quranic descriptions of different habitats and the harmonious way in which their inhabitants live within their ecosystems can be extrapolated to human beings. In other words we can explore how different human identities have been determined through living in diverse areas across cultures and races. The above verses also aimed to educate seventh-century society about the non-supremacy of the class system, with the Quran selectively addressing the inhabitants of the Arabian Peninsula. The main message was that we are all human beings, regardless of our origins. Interrelationship between human activity and human identity is analysed from the Quran in the next section of this search in the following manner.

All Quranic descriptions of human acts can be divided into three main groups

Identity Through Science, Philosophy and Artistic Concepts in the Quran

Table 1. The Quran's Description of Human Acts

Professions	Duty / Obligations	Prohibitions
1. Land 'Trade'	1. Obey God, and Law	1. Do not practice idolatry
2. Agriculture	2. Do justice	2. Adultery
3. Game-hunting	3. Look after the needy, orphans and old parents	3. Cheating
4. Sea merchant	4. Give women their share	4. Lewd acts
5. Poet	5. Innocent should not be charged	5. Do not fight against the cause of God
	6. Prayer (regular)	6. Traitor
	7. Purification	7. Hoarding, squandering
	8. Give your children and parents share of your property	8. Persecution, slandering
	9. Give right weight	9. Stealing, giving less weight
	10. Give just witness	10. Arrogance, transgression
	11. Fight for the cause of God	11. Impatience, hasty deeds
		12. Usury
		13. Killing each other (unless justified)
		14. Strong drink
		15. Chance game

- ❖ profession;
- ❖ duty and obligation; and
- ❖ prohibition.

The Quran does not specifically describe all the activities listed in Table 1, but the author feels that the meanings of many verses convey this idea. The sura references for Table 1 are given below:

(**1**) 2.273;16.6; 5.3; 2.164; 69.41; (**2**) 4.69; 4.58; 2.263; 2.215; 4.43; 2.177; 4.43; 2.177; 4.11; 6.153; (**3**) 6.152; 4.15; 10.23; 4.37; 2.190; 49.12; 75.31–40; 17.11; 3.130; 4.29; 2.219.

The human activities from the Bible can be grouped together in a similar way. The Bible includes many different professional activities, but only the relevant ones are mentioned in Table 2. All biblical references for this section (Table 2) are collectively numbered according to their biblical chapters. These are: Genesis (6.5–7; 9.6; 9.12, 13; 6.9, 22; 16.34); Exodus (15.26; 18.14, 15; 20.12; 23.10; 29.18); Leviticus (13.2–7; 14.35); and Mathew (7; 5.25; 22.37, 39).

Table 2. The Bible's Description of Human Acts

Professions	Duty / Obligations	Prohibitions
1. Carpenter, farmer	1. Obey God's order, be faithful and pure	1. Wickedness, lawlessness, and corruption
2. Builder	2. Do just, abstain evil	2. Killing of man by a man
3. Gift of skill (e.g. smith)	3. Be concerned with God's kingdom	
4. Priest	4. Love your enemy and the needy	

Using Quranic and biblical descriptions and guidance we can categorize occupations. These descriptions vary from that of habitats. Similarly, human activities provide description of the person's self. In the Quranic examples of the seventh-century Arabs the basis of their identity is their trades on land and sea, farming, game hunting and other activities such as poetry [125] [126] [127] [128]. This Old World knowledge has been conveyed to us not only through the Quran but also through the Bible.

The discussion at this stage reveals the bond that exists between human knowledge and activity. This bond holds together two separate strengths that attribute characteristics to an individual's identity. The first is knowledge, arising and expressed from within the human mind. The second is activity, evolving at first as an idea but then becoming a pursuit through the person's choice and action. Activities can be the daily chores of normal life, recreational or professional endeavours. It is worth reminding ourselves that activities may have a positive or a negative effect on the individual or the greater community. In the same way that we accept that there is a limitation on the lifespan of all life forms, we can assume that the number of activities that can be undertaken during their lives is also limited. As far as we are aware, no occupation or knowledge can be carried through beyond the boundaries of life into death.

The activity that is undertaken by individuals or groups is integral to their identity. For example, it can be said that Human 'A' lives for twenty years but follows a certain profession for only two years, whereas Human 'B' lives for forty years, and follows the same profession throughout his professional career. Hence Human B's experience could identify him as an expert in that line whilst A has too limited an experience to be identified as an expert. Similarly, a person's endeavour to improve his or her occupation also counts towards their professional identity. On the other hand, negligence, laziness and misconception through insufficient knowledge can become a drawback or limitation to one's occupational identity.

Before summing up the discussion on human activities, we need to look at some other views from the Quran, where mankind's activities are influenced by his or her character:

'time or Man'	(76.1)
'is impatient'	(70.19–21)
'is given to hasty deeds'	(16.36–37)
'misfortunes due to his deeds'	(42.30)

The above group of verses explains some of the limitations in human activity. The word **'time' or 'man'** (76.1) describes perfectly the age or period from birth to death of a human being. The author believes that in this instance the word time not only suggests the lifespan of a human but also links an individual's activities (occupational or otherwise) to his or her quality of life. The Quran tells us that **'hasty'** (16.36–37) deeds reflect an **'impatient'** (16.36–37) mind. This attitude may lead to failures in life. Also, when humans become negligent, lazy and unmindful towards their duty, they invite **'misfortunes'** (42.30), which arise from unaccomplished activities.

The author believes that mankind's power to plan and act accordingly makes him superior to other non-human life forms. However, the Quran has explained limited freedom in human activities and thoughts. The value of **'limited free will'** (36.58–68) is that it allows humans the option of performing their duties and achieving their goals. On the other hand even limited freedom can become a tool for destruction. This destructive process is brought about by humans through misuse or abuse of their power, as well as through unthoughtful or negligent activities.

BRIDGING THE GAP BETWEEN KNOWLEDGE AND ACTIVITY

Muslim Sufis believe that creation is a continuous process [129]. This idea of a continuous creative process combined with scientific endeavours to learn and interpret the facts of nature is the focus of this section. The author believes that the meaning of many of the verses in the Quran, which have been recited as divine messages but without proper understanding, can now be interpreted in a scientific context .

In the same way, modern scientists may need to rethink their approach on the basis of a faith-based science and find out whether or not this leads to scientific improvements in the twenty-first century [130]. The author believes that applying religious code for the pursuance of the *good* can bridge the gap between knowledge and activity.

So, how can the pursuit of knowledge bridge this gap between the two sides?

'increase knowledge – [with piety]' (20.114)

Knowledge has been referred to as a belief that is both true and justified, i.e. knowledge can be described as a relationship between a state of mind and a fact [131]. But the seeker of **'knowledge'** (20.114) has to make sure that the knowledge acquired is of benefit to humanity [132]. Limited access to knowledge or lack of understanding creates differences between individuals.

Robert Winston felt that the *human instinct* was spirituality beyond moral life [133]. This spirituality does not question whether an activity or thought is moral or amoral but accepts that the human instinct can perceive right from wrong. In other words humans have the capacity to make a moral choice [134] [135]. How we conduct ourselves on that basis determines our individual identity and differentiates us from those around us.

- 'every matter has its appointed time' (54.3)
- 'death is a must for every living being' (21.35)

These verses offer a reason for the lifetime attempt by some individuals to improve their identity through good intentions and activities before the **'appointed'** (54.3) time. Prophet Muhammad's (S:) saying 'you know best your own earthly matters' or *Ijtehad* [136] [137] not only gives strong support for understanding life but also for facing death.

This discussion has attempted to explore the relationship between the Quranic philosophies on creation, life and activity, and science. The realization that human identity is a term relative to an individual's existence, and that there are limitations to knowledge being acquired as well as the activities of individuals, brings into focus the difficulties of understanding this concept.

Conclusion

Islam has now become a global religion. Today's Islamic culture comprises ideas from different geographical backgrounds, numerous nationalities, a variety of languages and identities that are collectively combined within its faith to be universally known as the Muslim culture. Many Muslim philosophers, scientists and mathematicians have contributed to Islamic literature and knowledge in the past. Today again science offers explanations that can be related to Quranic ideas.

It can be concluded that many Quranic philosophies, when explained through modern terminologies, may become accessible to the layperson. The author hopes that the question of whether the passage of time might be a barrier to appreciating Quranic verses in the twenty-first century has been successfully rejected through this discussion.

At the same time it is explained that limitation in knowledge and activity in this mortal world contributes to self-recognition and interpretation of life. But can this search for identity or individuality of the human as a *specific* character be concluded at this stage? Can there be other relationships amongst living beings that qualify the status of humans as superior beings? The next chapter explores the possibility of such relationships.

Chapter Three

RELATIONSHIPS:
PLANTS, ANIMALS AND THE HUMAN SPECIES

In this section the author looks at how the Quranic philisophies deal with the concept of humans being superior to other living beings and how this might shape human identity.

'do not exceed limit' (6.141; 5.90)
'Allah's rules are in the middle path [practical ways]**'** (6.115)
'man benefits from created matters [in this case living matters]**'**
(22.65; 43.12–13)
'should not torture animals' (76.8; 33.72)
'communities like you, people like you' (45.3–6; 6.38)

The Bible echoes the same principles (Isa. 58.10).
According to the above verses there should be a harmonious balance between all living beings: **'do not exceed limit'** and **'man benefits from created matters'**. Can we really claim to be superior to other species such as plants and animals? Humans have no right to claim superiority over other living species unless we can prove that we surpass them in intelligence, techniques in survival, in adjustability to adverse surroundings, and especially in qualifying as a species that cares about life. We humans, despite having the intelligence to acquire knowledge

and the ability to pursue varied occupational activities, are still just another living being, and not necessarily the chosen or superior one, without rigorous proof.

The author suggests that human identity has to be formed in relation to other life forms on this planet. As mentioned in the previous chapters, the living process is a continuous flow of time and ceases only with death. We know that all living beings belong to a community and follow the pattern of birth, growth and death (Figure 3). This cyclical process replenishes the community with new members, allowing it to evolve, or in the absence of replenishment leading to its demise. In this discussion attempts are made to understand human identity in relation to non-humans and disadvantaged humans. When we form relationships or connect with other species, we create a bond that not only strengthens human association with other living communities but also contributes towards a harmonious natural order: **'Allah's rules are in the middle path** [practical ways]' (6.115).

HARMONIOUS EXISTENCE

In his book *Islam between East and West* (1989), Ahija A. Izetvegovic commented that the Quran repeatedly urges followers to meditate and observe or study life [138]. Meditation by prayer or contemplation helps to clarify our thoughts and reflects on life; whilst the observation and study of life, for example through scientific pursuits, help to expand our horizons. The author believes that in their own ways science and meditation have helped human society to push forward the frontiers of knowledge and understanding. The Quran specifies that knowledge should not only be applied to ourselves but also to our fellow beings (i.e. plants and animals) with whom we share this planet, as seen from **'communities like you, people like you'** (45.3–6; 6.38). This Quranic philosophy from fourteen hundred years ago gives us a glimpse of far-sightedness and echoes modern views on eco-friendly actions.

For many thousands of years humans have been aware of and have respected the communities of plants, animals and insects with whom they shared this planet. For ancient cultures such as the Australian Aborigines or the Native American Indians, all plants, animals and humans were accepted as interdependent [139] [140] [141], and therefore they lived in harmony and with respect for each other [142]. These cultures believed, and continue to believe, in a Supreme High Spirit or Being which takes care and keeps account of each act performed by community members. Unnecessary killing or violation of territory are still not allowed in these communities as humans are regarded as only part of a larger community.

However, unlike in ancient times, modern civilizations seem to have encouraged the growth of the selfish and demanding character of human beings. The simple rule of 'live and let others live' has largely been forgotten as the aggressive and greedy side of human nature has been allowed to flourish. Humans have used their linguistic power and the ability to assess and plan ahead to gain superiority, avoiding harm to themselves and gaining strength wherever possible. Their ability to find weakness in opponents, whether it is animals or other communities, or even amongst their own kind, has helped certain groups to establish power over less aggressive communities.

The fact that many instincts and behaviours associated with humans are also seen in animals and to some extent in plants is often overlooked. Scientific studies have shown that animals that live in communal groups have a common caring system and often hunt in packs. This shows communal behaviour that is beneficial for the growth and survival of the group. These characteristics are observed comprehensively in certain species such as elephants, whales, dolphins, apes and birds [143] [144] [145] [146] [147] [148] [149] [150] [151] [152]. Therefore the *fellow feeling* often associated only with humans also exists within other animal species. Then again, this does not exclude members of groups of animals from promoting individuality and even rivalry.

The above Quranic verses advise humans to show '[tolerance and] **not torture animals**' (76.8; 33.72) because that will be of **'benefit'** (22.65; 43.12–13) to all. They urge that humans **'should not exploit or exceed limit'** (6.141; 5.90) (i.e. the natural capacity of the planet) but live in harmony with other '[living] **communities**' (45.3–6; 6.38). We tend to overlook the contributions made by plants and animals in our daily life in providing food and other essential items. These items have not only helped to shape society but have been integral in the advancement of science, including a better understanding of medical science and the pharmaceutical industry, which is of great benefit to us. The question still remains whether humans have the capability to resist exploitation and live harmoniously with other communities (humans, plants and animals). If humans are unable to achieve these goals then can they claim themselves to be the most developed and intellectually superior life form?

The analysis so far shows that the human mind is capable of accepting and understanding the benefit of other communities and the importance of coexisting with them. But can humans today readily agree to share natural resources with other living beings (plants, animals and other humans)? And why should they? Perhaps we need to explore the logic behind these egalitarian ideas and apply them to all living beings.

HUMAN CAPABILITY

'Read' (96.1–5)

One of the most important insights that the Quran gives us regarding human identity is through the brain's capability to learn and evaluate; in fact, the first word of the first Quranic revelation to Prophet Muhammad (S:) was **'Read'** (96.1–5). From the very beginning the Quran has encouraged us to acquire knowledge.

Science tells us that the physical structure of man has not changed much since the time of *Homo erectus*, the first man to stand upright. However, the size of our brain has continued to grow from that time to its current mass [153] [154] [155]. In recent years, scientific studies conducted in America and Britain have shown that there is an area of the human brain responsible for religious or virtuous feelings [156] [157]. Scientists have identified an area situated in a site called the prefrontal lobe that is responsible for feelings of well-being. Therefore, to believe or to have faith and feelings of well-being towards oneself and others might have developed very early in human evolution. Perhaps the human mind had developed awareness of its surroundings and questioned its identity from the beginning of human history? Perhaps faith, which is regularly expressed through religious beliefs, has always been part of our thought process?

The first Quranic command, **'Read'** (96.1–5), can also be interpreted as elevating meditation and religious contemplation from acts of devotion to an intellectual status. Through this command the Quran revealed human superiority over other species because of our ability to pray or meditate as well as of our ability to acquire knowledge. These actions seem to be possible for humans since our brain is more developed [158] than that of other animals. The human brain can plan for its future and through education such plans can lead to a brighter future. Maybe the Quranic idea **'man benefits from created matters'** (22.65; 43.12–13) can also be applied to the human brain because it has been created with the power to read and offer a meaningful status to faith.

SHARING RESOURCES

In the Quran there are clear descriptions of the relationships between different living communities and nature. Certain names or descriptions (see below) related to living beings are cited in ways which make the symbiotic relationship between these natural processes and their life support systems clear. The idea of symbiosis, or life forms depending upon each other, whether human beings and plants or human beings and animals, is well known today. This special relationship was advocated by the Quran to improve the closeness between different species, and to nurture and protect the harmonious balance in nature. Religious scriptures in general have urged humans to preserve this relationship. Modern ecologists refer to this notion as having an *environmental consciousness*. The references from the Quran which are relevant to the idea of symbiosis within the human habitat can be divided into three sections:

1. Environmental or natural processes which contribute to the ecosystems of the living world.
2. Living species from non-human groups that may or may not be useful to humans but contribute to the human habitat.
3. Plant and animal products that are useful to humans.

In this respect the Bible echoes the same ideas as the Quran (Gen. 1.3; 1.14, 16, 19; 1.11,22).

1.
Names that are relevant to environmental or natural cycles which are mentioned in the Quran and are integral to the formation of the earth's atmosphere:

'sun and moon – day and night'	(13.2; 13.3)
'sky, stars [and] **– zodiacal signs'**	(65.12; 85.1)
'mountains with seven firmaments [or] **firm attachments – hills and stones'**	(13.3; 35.27, 28)
'sea, land, river, stream, and fountain'	(25.53; 16.15; 38.43)
'desert'	(9.90)
'wind, cloud – rain and water'	(51.1; 10.24)

2.
In the second category are examples of living species such as plants, animals, birds and insects which were known in the seventh-century Arabian Peninsula:

Plants and trees

'palm tree – Lote tree – Sidr tree'	(6.100; 53.14)
'banana, fig, pomegranates and dates'	(13.4; 56.29; 6.100; 13.4)
'olive, vine and vineyards'	(6.100; 18.32; 16.67)

'corns, buds of corn   – and cornfields'   (13.4; 6.99)
'seeds – and grains, herbs'   (6.99; 6.95)
'zanjabil [or] ginger – garlic, onion'   (76.17; 6.95)
'forest, woods, thicket – orchard, gardens, tufts'   (15.78; 80.28, 29; 19.60; 68.17; 101.5)
(for cucumber see ref. 43)

Names of animals, insects and birds

'apes – pig, dog, donkey, horse'
(5.60, 63; 5.63; 7.176; 62.5; 16.8)
'elephants – cattle – camel'   (105.1; 16.66; 88.17)
'cow, goat, sheep'   (2.67; 16.5)
'fish'   (35.12)
'ants – fly, bee'   (27.18; 22.73; 16.68)
'gnat'   (2.26)
'spider'   (29.41)
'Ababil [a small bird] **– birds of game'**   (2.57; 105.3; 5.5)
'Hoopoe [a large bird] **– quail'**   (27.20; 105.3)
'some creep on their bellies – [snake, worm. etc.]'   (24.45)

3.
    Plant and animal products useful to man in the seventh-century Arabian Peninsula:

'wine [to an extent as medicine] **– olive oil'**   (2.219; 23.20)
'wool – silk'   (101.5; 18.32)
'fibre [from palm leaf or] **rope'**   (111.5)
'fire from wood'   (56.71; 72)

The overwhelming message from these verses from the Quran is that earth is governed by the laws of nature with bountiful resources that may be used by humans and other living beings. The author believes that the harmonious cycles of life between, as well as within, living communities should not be destroyed if man wants to continue a compatible relationship with his environment. This kind of balanced relationship can only enhance man's *superior* status within nature.

Modern science likes to add detail on the genetic backgrounds of different beings through taxonomy, as this clarifies the variety and nature of the species concerned. Although the Quranic age had no language to describe exactly the names arising from such classifications, it nevertheless includes verses that could be relevant to modern science.

VARIETY IN NATURE, OR GENETICS?

'created variety among living animals and other living creatures' (6.100)
'some are the same but some are not' (6.99, 100)
'created different tastes in different fruits in the same soil – olive and dates' (23.19–21)
'created male and female in pairs. Created variations in man's language, colour and different nationalities' (2.213; 10.19)

These verses from the seventh-century Quran can be specifically linked to current scientific and social observations. When the Quran mentions creating **'variety'** (6.100) it is referring to the diversity observed in nature. Variety in nature creates differences, including in **'colour** [and] **language'** (2.213; 10.19), not only in the human race but also in other animals (and plants), and **'in taste'** (23.19–21) of fruits.

Scientists have elaborately studied differences in taste, colour and communication of sounds in animals, fruits and flowers. Now, genes, the smallest regulatory unit in living organisms, are known to carry coding systems for the production of amino acids, which combine to form a protein. So variations in the genetic code of the same amino acid, known scientifically as degeneration, will bring variation in the natural characteristics of an organism. Such changes are vital for adapting to changing environments and the propagation of species. These verses in the Quran, in a nutshell, direct us towards genetic variation, which science has shown to exist in all living groups.

The Quran says that both **'olive** and **dates'** are grown in the same soil, which was soaked in the same rain; still they differ **'in taste'** (23.19–21), indicating that they are genetically different species although they are products of the same environment. Similarly it mentions variation among animals: **'some are the same or alike and some are not and are different'** (6.100). This may be referring to genetic variations between different animal species and also variation within the same species. So when breeding occurs between two members of the same species, similarities and variations within genes from each parent will most likely produce offspring with a combination of similarities and differences with respect to the parents.

When the Quran mentions **'created pairs of male and female'** (6.99; 100), it signifies that each belongs to a different gender with variations in their basic physical compositions and structures. The notion of genetic variations in man and the consequences of such variations are found in verses from the Quran on different human characteristics such as '[skin] **colour – languages** [and] **nationalities'** (2.213; 10.19). The consequences of genetic variation in man are not only of medical interest but are also important for tracing human genealogy and anthropology.

BIOSPHERE

'purity, harmony and law drive away evil'	(30.3)
'Allah established harmony'	(79.29)

What is the relationship between **'purity, harmony and law'** and nature? The above verses clearly show that without harmonious existence the balance in nature's infrastructure may fall apart. Humans, the most capable of all created species, play a major role in maintaining this harmony as and when they use natural resources with good intention. The reference to **'law – evil'** (30.3) is an indication that human need, or indeed greed, ought to be limited so that the natural world, including plants and animals, may be sustained. Only through a sharing and benevolent attitude can man limit the damage done to nature. Although plants and animals adapt to a changing environment for survival, they are unable to plan for the future and do not profit from their circumstances.

In this section the Quranic teaching on symbiosis or interdependence between different living groups and the effect of atmosphere, water cycle and domestic environment will be discussed. Quranic descriptions of the sun, moon, cloud, rain, mountains and human life are grouped together in a way that helps us to make sense of our atmosphere. The natural environment around us seems to be the most suitable habitat for human growth and the Quran gives us an understanding of it in the context of human life. Through our appreciation of nature we have an incentive to preserve our surroundings, where man and other living beings together create the universe or biosphere.

Verses from the Quran in this category have been divided into three sections:

1. Atmosphere.
2. Earth's surface and water cycle.
3. The development of environmental niches for plants, animals and humans.

1.
Atmosphere

'created stars and constellations are for you, to guide you in the darkness of land and sea' (6.97)

'behold! In the creation of the heavens and the earth; in the alterations of the night and the day; in the sailing of the ships through the ocean for the profit of mankind' (2.164)

'do they not look at the sky above them? How We [Allah and His majestic power] **have made it and adorned it, and there are no flaws in it?'** (21.31, 32; 40.46, 64; 51.47)

The above verses give some examples from the Quran that establish the connection between living communities and the atmosphere. For example, the polar star in the northern sky remains in a fixed position, whilst other celestial bodies move slowly and change direction according to the season. Travellers by land and sea, including Arabian merchants and sailors [159], have used the polar star for thousands of years to determine their routes in the darkness. Recent studies have shown that even migratory birds flying through the night use stars and the light of the polar star [160].

2.
Earth's Surface and Water Cycle

'and the earth we have spread it out' (55.3–13)
'and set thereon mountains standing firm' (21.31)

It was mentioned earlier (see Chapter 2, ref. 113) that according to the Quran mountain tops remain standing **'firm'** (21.31) on the earth's surface and that their roots are deeply embedded under the topmost crust of the earth. Modern geological studies agree with this idea of roots holding mountains down firmly on the surface of the earth. Humans and other life forms enjoy and use mountainous areas as a special habitat.

'the wind is forcing the cloud from the sea' (25.48)
'and then the cloud drops the rain on the field' (25.48)

'the cloud has measured amount of raindrops in it and in true proportions' (2.19, 20; 23.18)
'and We send down from the sky rain charged with blessing' (25.48)

The Bible reflects almost the same idea as the above Quranic verses (Isa. 51.13; 55.9, 10).

Knowledge of the water cycle, as described in the above Quranic verses, has informed Muslims through the ages of how the wind rises from the sea and creates clouds that contain **'measured amount of raindrops … in true proportions'** (2.19, 20; 23.18) (see also Chapter 2). They also show the vital role which mountains and wind play in the formation of cloud and rain. **'Rain charged with blessing'** (25.48) can be taken as an example where after rainfall the earth blooms with green and other colours.

These descriptions in the Quran of the recycling of water through evaporation, condensation and rainfall, with each water molecule showing a precise chemical composition, and the wind or airflow systems and natural barriers such as mountains playing a central role in the creation of rainfall, are comprehensive. In fact, scientific studies and depictions of the water cycle match closely those in the Quran.

3.

Domestic Environment of Plants, Animals and Humans

'in the rain which God sends down from the skies, and the life which He gives [therewith to an] **earth that is dead'** (2.19, 20)
'Allah created life from water, created plants and creepers' (21.30)
'in the beasts of all kinds that He scatters through the earth' (15.12–14)
'rain from the sky: from it you drink, and out of it [grows] **the vegetation on which you feed your cattle'** (23.19)

These Quranic verses remind us that life rarely survives without water, light or air except in special circumstances, and these components are vital for life, its growth and sustenance. The vast majority of living creatures including plants perform the same biological processes, known as metabolism and respiration, to survive. Water is an essential component of both metabolism and aerobic respiration, or respiration in the presence of oxygen. Plants, animals and humans share these earthly resources which we have inherited. The Quranic philosophy that **'rain – and the life which He gives – rain from the sky: from it you drink, and out of it** [grows] **the vegetation on which you feed your cattle'** (2.19, 20) (23.19) is scientifically accurate. The flourishing of vegetation and animals in the presence of water, and the withering of life in its absence, demonstrate its importance to life.

The above verses emphasize that fourteen hundred years ago the Quran was trying to reinforce in human minds the nature of interdependence or symbiosis amongst the living communities. It is important to note the overlap of the messages **'Allah's rules are in the middle path'** (6.115), i.e. realistic ways in which the limits are not exceeded, and **'man benefits from created** [living] **matters'** (22.65; 43.12–13). The symbiotic relationship of man with his surroundings or with other communities is a central part of our identity and man is urged to stay within sensible limits during such interactions.

It is worth asking who the members of these other communities are, and whether they should be mentioned along with humans. The Quran's answer is given in the next section.

LIVING COMMUNITIES OR INHABITANTS OF THE PLANET EARTH

'God has provided Adam's children with wholesome things and exalted them above many of His creatures' (17.70)
'all living things have their own communities. There is not an animal on the earth nor a being that flies on its wings, but forms communities like you. They are people like you. Allah has given different backgrounds for different varieties.' (6.38; 6.99)

'Allah established harmony' (79.29)
'Man is gifted with faculties like speech, vision, taste, knowledge' (21.92, 93; 16.78; 23.78)

When applied to mankind, **'communities'** (6.38; 6.99) relate to societies, whether they are immediate or geographic neighbours, where there is kinship based on common cultural and/or religious characteristics. Ecologically a community is understood to be a group of interdependent plants and animals inhabiting the same region. In the above Quranic verse **'communities like you'** indicates group structures in living creatures, which would be denoted scientifically as species that live, grow, behave, reproduce and die in the same manner and share the same environment.

According to the Quran, members of the same species, whether animals or birds, have their own group, which adapts to a particular ecosystem. So, for example, some plants of the same species may grow tall whilst others remain bushy. These ideas are concurrent with scientific hypothesis such as Darwin's theory of species and survival of the fittest [161], according to which different species adapt to different ecological situations to survive competition. For example, the human species has been **'gifted with faculties'** (21.92, 93; 16.78; 23.78) of speech from the area in the brain that forms words, which enables them to communicate not only for survival, or for harbouring community relationships, but also for advancing the frontiers of knowledge.

The Quranic idea of **'they are people like you'** (6.38; 6.99) gives the impression of a family structure with human-like behaviour. It suggests a family comprising a mother, a father and a child or children, in which parents look after their offspring, build a resting place, share food, show love, guidance and care for each other. Now, scientists in this century, as well as the last, have gathered evidence showing that nurturing is a strong natural instinct in birds and animals for the propagation of their species. There is no doubt that members of the same species not only communicate with each other but also care for each other. It has been already mentioned that some important community characteristics have been observed by scientists in certain animals [see refs 145; 146; 147; 148; 149; 150; 151 and 152]. Such complex communal structures exist where different members within the social strata perform different duties, such as hunting, nursing, grooming and even mourning their dead relatives (as seen in herds of elephants), which are comparable with behaviour in human society.

The same verse can also be analysed from a different angle. We can try to understand the message **'they are people** [communities or nationals] – **like you'** (6.38; 6.99) in terms of biological make-up. Several genome-sequencing projects for sequencing DNA, life's protein-coding molecule, from members of the bacterial, plant and animal kingdom, which includes humans, have recently been completed. The results have shown that approximately 95 per cent or more of human DNA has similarities with that of higher apes, and even large components of the bacterial genome are conserved within higher life forms such as apes and humans [162]. This illustrates that all life forms share some common biological components or processes for living, which are encoded into their genes.

Studies on memory show that all kinds of memories lie hidden within the brain, until something triggers these dormant events to surface as remembrance [163] [164] [165]. David Attenborough in his documentary on birds showed how the bower bird builds its display bowers. In this case the bird's memory and capability to replicate the bower in an exact manner shows that an inherent knowledge is present within the bird [166]. The finding that the DNA of the big apes is closely related to that of humans, as well as the bower bird's instinctive reproduction of the display bower, could reflect the words from the Quran, **'people like you'** (6.38; 6.99).

The idea of **'different backgrounds'** (6.38; 6.99) can also be interpreted in several ways. It has been confirmed that different animals communicate differently. All animal groups (communities) that have been studied scientifically have been shown to display certain cultural activities that are limited to their species. For example, animals like the elephants show respect for their dead by standing and touching the carcass and/or bones. Chimpanzees and baboons can usually guess what other members in the group are thinking [167]. Birds are well known for using tools to acquire food or for making comfortable decorative nests for their chicks.

The author has already discussed how plants [168] [169] adapt to their surroundings, but can this be assumed to be intelligence or foresight in plants or is it just adaptation for survival? Although it is true that plants do not show motion in the same way as animals, they have certain capabilities that are lacking in animals. Plants can sense things and have been shown to respond to light, temperature, moisture content and even sound [170]. Over time they can also change their leaf pattern (variegated or plain) and size, scent and colour of flowers, and methods of pollination. These qualities in plants could reflect intelligent behaviour [171]. Therefore, as stated in the Quran and corroborated by science, intelligent behaviour shown by groups of plants and animals, whether for survival or for cultural reasons, varies from species to species and can be thought of as the product of their physical and cultural environment, i.e. **'different backgrounds'** (6.38; 6.99).

In the verse **'man is gifted with faculties like speech, vision, taste, knowledge'** (21.92, 93; 16.78; 23.78) we observe the mention of certain traits which together help mankind to attain wisdom and achievement. Each of these qualities helps surpass and upgrade human capability for survival in nature, at the same time making man a superior being, enabling him to dominate others. Since research suggests that only the human brain can look to the future and plan, possibly because of mankind's more evolved physical, intellectual and cultural backgrounds [172] [173], it would support the above verse, **'gifted with faculties'**.

There are certain inborn and other acquired qualities in humans that give us a sense of superiority. The verse expressing **'different backgrounds'** (6.38; 6.99) is aptly used to explain inter-species cultural differences, whilst the word **'gift**[ed]**'** (21.92, 93; 16.78; 23.78) can be taken to signify a present, which is lovingly presented to the recipient. **'Wisdom** [or] **knowledge'**, which raises the human status above that of any other living species in this natural world, is expressed through this verse, and therefore needs to be appreciated as such.

At this point in time, man can claim to be superior amongst (known) life forms. But can we hold on to that status for ever? What about man's natural domain? How has that been defined by God? The author examines these themes in the next section.

HUMAN USE OF NATURE AND MAN'S NATURAL UNIVERSE

'let man reflect the food he eats: how We bring forth the corn, the grapes and the fresh vegetation, – olive and the palm the thickets, the fruits of different tastes, trees and the green pastures for you and for your cattle' (23.19–21)

'Allah created cattle whereupon ye ride, use some for burden, some for their skin and some for your food' (16.58)

'in the cattle – drink which is in their belly, pure milk palatable to the drinker' (16.69)

'from the belly of bees comes forth a syrup of different hues, a cure for men' (16.69)

'God has provided Adam's children with wholesome things and exalted them above many of His creatures' (17.70)

'purity, harmony and law drives away evil' (30.3)

The fact that man is dependent on different living communities for his survival is a common theme in the above verses. Whatever their source, items are procured from plants and animals, including insects such as bees, for food and drink, making man dependent on them. Conversely, man has also helped both plants and animals to survive within their natural environment through planned agricultural activities and animal husbandry.

The list of vegetation in the Quran, ranging from crops and grains to fresh fruits and vegetables, give us an idea of the produce found in seventh-century Arabia. Some of this might have come from neighbouring countries through trade. The above verses give a detailed description of different uses of domestic cattle. The author feels that the Quranic reference to cattle includes cows, goats, horses, lambs, camels and donkeys, which were all common to the Arabian Penninsula. The use of these **'cattle whereupon ye ride, use some for burden, some for their skin and some for your food'** (16.58) and various other practical purposes has been cited in the Quran. The idea of **'wholesome things – like pure milk – from the belly of bees comes forth a syrup'** (17.70; 16.69) of different colours (see also Chapter 1) shows the relationship between humans and other animals.

These verses also reflect the fact that God has made the earth acquiescent to man, since **'man benefits from created** [living] **matters'** (22.65; 43.12–13) and **'God has provided Adam's children with wholesome things and exalted them above many of His creatures'** (17.70). So this confirms man's status amongst other living matters, i.e. he has been granted a place over others. However, the Quran also warns mankind to respect nature's boundaries **'with purity, harmony and law'** (30.3) and not destroy the benefits bestowed by the natural world. The message **'let man reflect'** (23.19–21) adds further caution on the same note.

MAN'S DOMINANCE OVER OTHERS

'Allah taught man how to dominate over other creatures and how to utilize other powers on this earth' (16.78)
'Allah subdued the ocean, so that you may eat of its fresh fish and bring up valuables from its depth – all become subservient to man by Allah's – command' (16.14)
'Allah created man to serve Him, and to be His representative on e arth' (21.92, 93)

The above Quranic verses show that Allah has granted a higher status for humans above other life forms by making man **'serve Him, and to be His representative on earth'** (21.92, 93), whereas making other living beings **'subservient'** (16.14) to man. Humans have acquired wisdom by learning from past mistakes and by understanding how to plan ahead. As mentioned earlier, the author believes that human superiority or the ability to **'dominate over other creatures'** (16.78) comes from man's knowledge and power, as well as from his limited freedom to choose. This is gained through **'faculties like vision, hearing, speech and knowledge'** (21.92, 93; 16.78; 23.78), i.e. detailed thinking and planning that only the human brain has the capacity for. The human brain has acquired knowledge through its ability to think, read and write, while the powers of touch, speech and vision have allowed man to communicate. Man's ability to accommodate and adjust to adversities through planning for the future has also placed him above other living creatures.

The Bible echoes the idea that 'gift of skill is from God' (Exod. 28.3), indicating that man should use his power responsibly.

In the next section, the discussion focuses on the Quran's insight into human shortcomings and the verses act as warnings as well as a reminder to mankind.

A REMINDER OF MAN'S LIMITATIONS

'Allah the Creator of all, sustains all'	(7.54)
'Allah's spirit breathed into man'	(15.2)
'limited freedom in choice and action'	(36.58–68)
'Allah does not love wasters'	(6.141)

Nowhere in the Quran do we find the **'spirit of Allah – breathed'** (15.2) into any other creature other than humans. The author believes that reference to the **'spirit'** of Allah could be to the power that has been bestowed upon man through **'limited freedom'** (36.58–68), allowing him to make the choices and decisions necessary for life. Knowledge gathered through such action helps to shape and protect man's future whilst ensuring that he learns of his limitations through such experiences.

The verse Allah **'sustains all'** (7.54) probably indicates that as the Creator of the whole of creation He has perfected His systems of life and its processes in cyclical periods, providing each system with essential necessities for survival in its environment. Their ways of acquiring food, building a resting place, caring for their offspring and finally dying to enable growth of the new generation are all part of the cyclical nature of life. Therefore the reference to **'sustains all'** (7.54) indicates the creative source, which nurtures old and new, human and non-human lives, from the beginning to the end; i.e. the evolution of a 'being' from its birth to its demise and all the intermediate stages. As mentioned earlier, plants can deliberately move towards a light source, or towards support, to grow. Animals have more capability in this matter. For example, animals can sense danger and move away from it; cats and dogs show instinctive likes or dislikes towards their friends and foes. But complete freedom and a range of thoughtful acts to modify the future are not seen in non-human species.

Man's actions are not only physical but also mental. Often greed and wastefulness are consequences of human actions, and the Quran warns that **'Allah does not love wasters'** (6.141). One of the prominent factors that demarcates between the deprived and the extravagant communities in the world is **'waste'** due to human wealth. Man achieves wealth through his or her freedom of choice in planning and action, whereas wastefulness demonstrates arrogance and negligence in the individual and society.

Arrogance pushes the boundary of self-recognition and self-condemnation by humans, as shown by the following series of Quranic verses on the darker side of human beings, which tries to set boundaries for human behaviour and offers man a chance to rectify his poor actions.

THE DARKER SIDE OF HUMAN BEINGS

'man plots against his own soul'	(6.123; 10.44)
'man's misfortune is due to his own deed'	(44.15)
'man's arrogance'	(17.31, 32)
'transgresses all bounds'	(96.6–14)
'transgresses insolently'	(10.23–24)
'is impatient and grudging'	(17.19–21)
'is given to hasty deeds'	(21.37)

'causes cruelty to animals' (16.58)
'man's duty to dumb animals is to look after them, feed them and house them properly' (76.8)
'[man] **wastes excess**' (7.31; 5.90)
'Lo! Allah enjoined justice and kindness' (11.90)
'man's growth and activity depend on God and his Honour depends on his righteousness' (39.70)

The above verses make it clear that mankind can be prone to cruelty to animals, and other misdeeds. Similarly, certain Hadiths from the life of Prophet Muhammad (S:) also note these qualities in man and serve as warnings:

- the Prophet Muhammad (S:) was angry with someone who cut a chicken's limb while it was still alive [174];
- the Prophet warned Muslims about their attitude towards the slaughtering of animals, and asked them to show their kindest manner [175];
- the Prophet said '… do not withhold water that is superfluous, for that will prevent people from grazing their cattle' [176];
- save water, it is for thirsty creatures [177].

Regarding man's behaviour, the Bible says that 'satisfy the famished creature' (Isa. 58.10), 'be concerned with the kingdom of God' (Matt. 6.33).

These verses from the Quran and the Bible, as well as the Hadiths, describe some of the ways in which man can act thoughtlessly towards animals, as well as certain behaviour (e.g. arrogance) that characterizes the darker side of man. The author believes that such actions may be unique to mankind and arise from the misuse of his **'limited free will'** and the ability to **'act with choice'** (36.58–68).

Shams Un Nahar Zaman

THE CONSEQUENCES OF MAN'S ACTIONS

'Allah created everything in harmonious existence'	(30.20–27)
'Allah's rules are in the middle path [practical]**'**	(6.115)
'Lo! Allah enjoined justice and kindness'	(11.90)
'human heart, eyes and ears fail to grasp the truth'	(7.149)
'man's misfortune is due to his own deeds'	(44.15)

Human dominance over other creatures can only be harmonious if humans show a sense of justice and control. We are advised upon the ideal choices for mankind through the above Quranic verses: **'Allah created everything in harmonious existence'** and **'Allah's rules are in the middle path'**, i.e. choices which are balanced, practical and do not exceed the limit. Man should not only benefit from natural resources but should also be the main influence in enhancing natural wealth from plants, animals and other resources.

In other words, humans need to look after living beings and the natural world so that our mutually beneficial attitude preserves the superior status bestowed upon mankind and secures our future. For example, human greed has been driving the continuous extraction and exploitation of natural resources such as forests for wood. The resulting felling of trees, often without replanting, will erode the soil's natural fertility, giving rise to deforestation, soil erosion, even landslides and desertification [178]. These processes, which are already apparent in many parts of the world, such as Africa and South America, affect the moisture content in the atmosphere, which in turn affects rainfall and soil fertility.

Lack of rain in many parts of sub-Saharan Africa, due to climate change, has resulted in crops failing, leading to famine. Similarly, an increase in floods due to tidal waves (e.g. tsunamis) has resulted in destruction and famine. These are also recent events that have probably been accelerated owing to man's actions [179] [180]. Furthermore, the pollution of air, water and soil, largely from human activities, has also caused an imbalance in the ecosystem globally. During a visit to China in 2005 the author saw the encroachment of large industrial and urban living areas where farmlands used to feature on the shore of the Yangtze river. This urbanization and industrialization process has displaced farmers, often into concrete apartments quite far from their lands, and has polluted the river. Moreover, it has resulted in the cutting down of trees and bushes on the banks of the Yangtze.

This type of activity will no doubt bring ecological as well as social changes in these regions in the future but may also lead to environmental catastrophes [181]. In autumn 2006, the Chinese government had to demolish a dam on the Yangtze, at a cost of millions of yuan, because it caused so much disruption to the surrounding areas. These events are but a few examples of how the Quranic verse **'man's misfortune is due to his own deed'** (44.15) can be confirmed.

In the same way exploitation of farm animals such as cattle or poultry for an ever growing and demanding meat market with high-intensity animal breeding and unnatural diets has resulted in a fall in meat quality. Additionally, we have seen the emergence of diseases such as mad cow disease and its human form, Creutzfeldt-Jakob disease. Exploitation of wild animals, e.g. the use of bush meat in African markets, which is exported globally, has also been detrimental to human health. It is hypothesized that the human immunodeficiency virus [182] was acquired from eating bush meat, in particular monkey brains. Man will do anything to survive as well as to make a profit, and will not hesitate to destroy rare species of plants and animals in the process [183]. Such exploitation has not only been detrimental for the species concerned but has also affected man now and will continue to do so in the future through depletion of his natural habitat as the **'human heart, eyes and ears fail to grasp the truth'** (7.149).

Therefore, as the Quranic verses suggest, interference by man, whether it be for agriculture or animal husbandry, should not disturb the natural balance to the extent that it damages the **'harmonious existence'** (30.20–27) between nature and man. For instance, in the past many tribal and aboriginal communities had evolved infrastructures to reflect their natural ecosystems. Maybe our twenty-first-century lifestyles should be modified to reflect a better management of our environment? Although humans have the right to control their ecological inheritance, some of which has taken millions of years to evolve, they need to apply the **'middle path'** (6.115) in order to enjoy a sustainable future.

The Quran tells us of the consequences of ignoring these warnings in the next section.

WARNINGS

'do not exceed [limit]' (5.90; 6.141)
'is greedy and negligent [towards orphans and the poor]' (75.31, 32)

The Quran extensively promotes natural harmony on earth and, as already discussed, this is a reminder to help conserve the natural world and the ecosystem. Since humans know how to balance the use of natural resources without exploiting it, the Quranic warning **'not to exceed** [limit]' (5.90; 6.141) is not out of place. These verses, although not often heeded, are there to help man coexist harmoniously with nature without becoming **'greedy'** (75.31, 32) and intolerant.

According to the Quran preservation of a harmonious natural system also includes maintaining harmony within human society. In the Quran able-bodied members of the community are encouraged to look after rather than be **'negligent** [towards orphans and the poor]' (75.31, 32). A society that neglects its dependants and less able members creates a social burden and unhappiness which may eventually erode social order and harmony. A study carried out in Great Britain in April 2007 reported that 25 per cent of children in Britain were living below the poverty line. However, how many people think about this issue and its consequences? Archbishop Desmond Tutu captured the essence of providing social empathy in his comment 'what we need is compassionate love, only through this kind of emotion and activity can a person prove what he or she is like' [184].

'to Him is the goal, to Him is the return' (28.70)
'human heart, eyes and ears fail to grasp the truth' (7.149)

At present many different organizations and charities in the UK, such as the NSPCC, the RSPCA, Age Concern and the World Wide

Fund for Nature, demand equal rights for children, animals, the aged, the disabled and the environment, respectively [185]. Such organizations, many of which are global, try to redress the natural balance and harmony which have often been destroyed by human action (power and politics), corroding both our society and the environment in which we live. If we act too late in redressing and analysing our actions then the verse **'to Him is the goal, to Him is the return'** (28.70) helps man to remember that one day we will be judged for our lack of action.

Therefore the modern concept of human identity needs to consider man's relationship with or concern for neighbouring communities, both human and non-human, to establish a sense of harmony.

Conclusion

The Quranic verses discussed in this chapter promote harmonious existence using the **'middle path** [practical ways]**'** (6.115) and indicate its **'benefits'** (43.12–13) to man. Indeed, we should conserve the environment and care for other living creatures that share our ecosystem not only because it gives us a sustainable habitat but also because without such coexistence the planet would become impoverished and environmentally more unsound. The author believes that every individual has to approach the question of such relationship **'with purity, harmony and law'** (30.3), and that individual effort should be reflected across the community. A harmonious balance in society, comprising different communities which are not **'exceeding limit'** (5.90; 6.141), can help the environment remain tranquil. The quality of the relationship between humans and those who are orphans, poor or needy, as well as other non-humans, is becoming more important and needs to be handled with care. Lastly, the author believes humans will acquire a superior status only if they tread the **'middle path'** (6.115). But then the question arises of whether humans as individuals or in a group can claim this title of superiority? Is everybody the same? Could there be differences between one human being and another which will enable some to be more superior than others?

Chapter Four

PHILOSOPHY:
UNITY AND DIVERSITY IN HUMANS

The theme of this chapter is whether qualities that make a person different from others still make them acceptable to society.

UNDERSTANDING VARIABILITY IN HUMAN NATURE

'only Allah creates and holds all records, – some known, some not known' (10.20; 16.8, 12; 27.75; 31.20; 72.26; 77)
'some are the same and some are different' (6.99, 100)
'Allah has given different backgrounds for different varieties' (30.22; 2.213; 10.19)

When the above group of Quranic verses is used to analyse human nature, the discussion becomes more philosophical than scientific. This is mainly because, despite any perceived feelings of 'us' and 'them', a concept of *social cohesiveness* seems to exist in communities. If, according to the above verses, we accept that some people belong to the **'same'** and **'known'** group as us whilst others are part of **'different'** and **'not** known' groups, then we can begin to understand the effort that may or may not be needed for multicultural societies to coexist. In other words, what do persons of **'different backgrounds'** (30.22; 2.213; 10.19) need to contribute for an unified modern society to function?

Humans invariably identify with familiar surroundings, creating a feeling of 'us', which may be reflected in our emotional or behavioural expressions, economic status, cultural beliefs or even our daily routines. As expressed by the above Quranic verses, these are part of the human nurturing process and are separate from nature, or the genetic components that differentiate individuals.

'O lord increase my knowledge [with piety]' (20:114)

According to Quranic philosophy **'knowledge** [with piety]', which broadens the horizon of human vision and action, through tolerance and understanding, also helps to develop a self-assured identity in humans. According to both religious texts and scientific studies on human behaviour, we have evolved with certain contrasting qualities, such as morality and selfishness [186]. Therefore, by studying Quranic opinions in conjunction with scientific knowledge, we should be able to identify how characteristics such as morality and selfishness affect human nature. According to the author, discussions on human individualism will identify some of the main characteristics that separate one individual from another. In fact, science has recently identified a location within the human brain that recognizes and differentiates self from non-self [187] [188]. This discovery helps to explain and rationalize human behaviour, and complements the Quranic verses on variability or **'different background'** (30.22; 2.213; 10.19) in humans.

Interestingly, Fazlur Rahman (1984) has observed that a major problem for Muslims of the post-modern era is the lack of contemporary cultures through which to understand their holy book [189]. According to him, Islam covers a comprehensive range of topics and has a more direct relationship to life than other religions [190]. He urges Muslims to modernize the boundaries of Islam. Modernization of an individual or a community comes through education, and as such broadens the horizon of their understanding.

Therefore we need to understand how the knowledge and wisdom from the Quran can be brought into contemporaneous Muslim society. In the twenty-first century our lifestyles are highly interwoven with scientific developments. Unless one has some knowledge of science, he or she cannot interpret the Quranic messages in the context of modern life [191]. At the same time modern science is gradually advancing towards a philosophical consciousness whereby the scientific world is considering whether or not to apply morality with its advances. Some pioneers are asking the question whether *good science* or *bad science* should be pursued [192].

In terms of the Quran, Bruce Lawrence (2006) has reflected that its meanings are multilayered [193]. In previous discussions we have shown how principles and wisdom from the Quran have served human needs through the ages. The Quran, in effect, acts as a store of knowledge which is accessible to all humans and brings well-being to all communities. It helps in the realization of self, making the faithful humble, knowledgeable and self-assured. The Quran also teaches tolerance, understanding and acceptance of variations (different opinions, races, etc.) in others.

DIFFERENCES IN EMOTIONAL EXPRESSIONS

'contemplate and understand'	(3.190, 191; 17.45–48)
'some are the same and some are different'	(6.99; 100)
'knowledge comes through inspiration'	(6.106)

Religious teachings assert that God has given us His grace not only as love, but also as wisdom [194], whilst science argues that it develops change and wisdom through revolution [195]. Following this argument it can be said that all branches of science including medical science have revolutionized the modern world through research. Its findings of a strong link between our body and mind give us the opportunity to argue that the same fundamental source which gave us love has also bestowed us with wisdom.

In fact, our inherited qualities are among the most important factors which mould the physical and mental characteristics of different individuals. However, according to medical studies humans differ from one another at even the molecular level. The DNA molecule in the human cell nucleus (it is the code for the body's building blocks and is found within each cell) is the simplest unit of chemical compound that codes our characteristics [196] [197] [198] [199]. It contains the genetic information that helps to make each of us an individual person. Genes are individual units within the genome which carry bits of information that switch *on* and *off* when required, like trains arriving at and departing from a station. In contrast the genome is a multi-task centre, such as a railway station, which makes up the whole system.

Science also tells us that the DNA double-helix structure remains wrapped around a special protein known as a histone [200]. This protein and others control expression of the gene units that code different chemical activities or enzymes. We know that the genetic code for each gene, and the genome, is inherited from both parents and can form a unique combination in the progeny. So our individual quality is expressed, to a large extent, according to the order of our chemical composition. Perhaps a simple diagram will explain how the human DNA operates in controlling emotional expressions from the moment of perception to the release of emotion (see Figure 4). The diagram shows that humans express emotion in different ways. However, emotion can be controlled and it is thought that knowledge and faith can help. Scientific research has found that determination, perseverance and repetition can help to control and change our emotional states [201] [202]. This scientific finding compares well with the Quranic advice **'contemplate and understand'** (3.190; 191; 17.45–48).

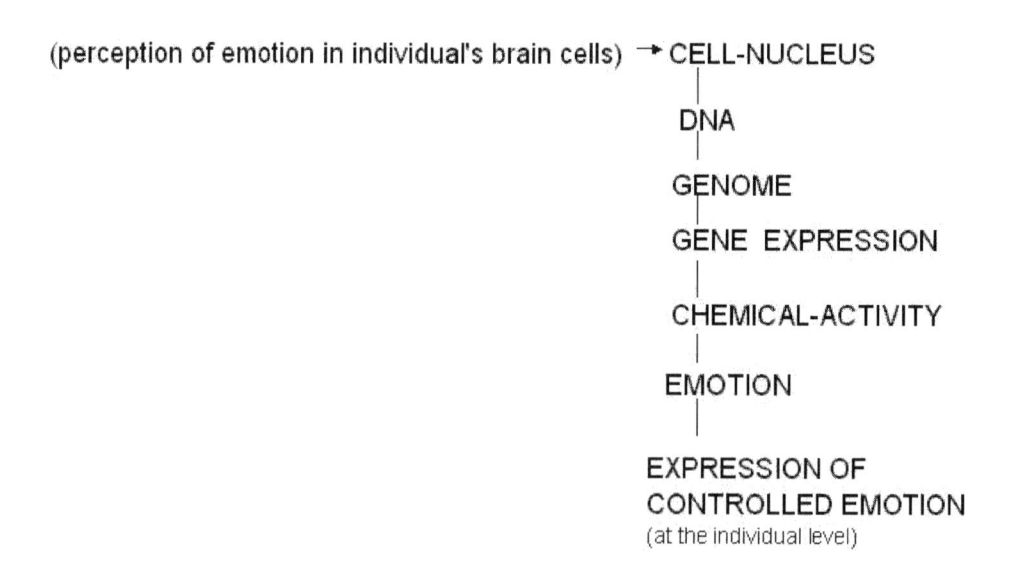

```
(perception of emotion in individual's brain cells) → CELL-NUCLEUS
                                                         |
                                                        DNA
                                                         |
                                                      GENOME
                                                         |
                                                   GENE EXPRESSION
                                                         |
                                                   CHEMICAL-ACTIVITY
                                                         |
                                                      EMOTION
                                                         |
                                                   EXPRESSION OF
                                                   CONTROLLED EMOTION
                                                   (at the individual level)
```

Figure 4. Human emotional path.

The discussion so far has pointed us to the Quranic idea of **'some are the same and some are different'** (6.99, 100). Although scientifically no two individuals possess identical DNA they may have similar DNA, as between a parent and a child. So we can postulate that the above Quranic word, **'same'**, indicates the nearest biological and intellectual match. This may explain why we develop into different people even when we live in the same family and in the same environment.

We know that the Quran encourages us to **'read'** and learn **'by the pen'** to acquire knowledge (96.1–5), and tells us that **'knowledge comes through inspiration'** (6.106). Now inspiration accounts for emotional involvement in the learning process, as emotion originates in the mind (which is the functioning part of the brain [203]) and is closely followed by feelings. In this way our different ways of learning, understanding and expressing our views also help us to become different individuals.

DIFFERENCES IN APTITUDE AND ATTITUDE TO LEARNING

'Man is gifted with faculties like speech, vision, taste, knowledge' (21.92, 93; 16.78; 23.78)

Mankind has the advantage over larger animals because we can articulate and formulate plans through **'speech, vision, taste, knowledge'** (21.92, 93; 16.78; 23.78) and accumulate knowledge through the process of learning. Of course, learning is one of the most important functions controlled by our brain [204]. In order to explain the complex processes which make up our mind and body the author has given below a simple description of the scientific process.

In response to a flash of light 10 billion brain nerve cells (neurons) become active and act together in a coordinated manner, as nerve cells are a vast network [205] [206]. During the learning process, the brain's nerve cells create impulses of electric current, and coded information is then passed through the long tails of nerve cells called axons in the neural network [207]. These long tails react at a junction called a synapse and transmit electrical impulses. These impulses carry messages around the body at a speed of up to 120 metres a second [208]. Importantly, functioning cells are able to cross gaps and send information through electrical impulses between neurons via synaptic gaps [205].

A simplified scheme of the activities of the human brain during the learning and memorization process is given in Figure 5. When the original idea or thought is added to a new idea or inspiration, the process initiates new electrical impulses, which through several functional steps create the process of thought that allows the mind to grasp new ideas and to learn. Ability of the mind to acquire a new idea varies from person to person. The mind can master new skills through concentration and can be trained for a variety of intellectual work.

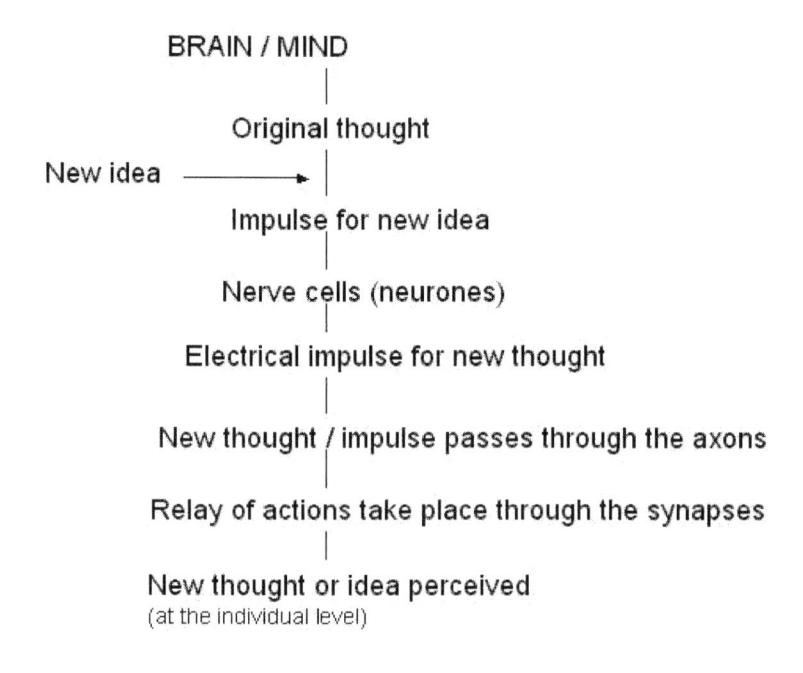

```
                    BRAIN / MIND
                         |
                    Original thought
       New idea  ─────────▶|
                    Impulse for new idea
                         |
                    Nerve cells (neurones)
                         |
                    Electrical impulse for new thought
                         |
               New thought / impulse passes through the axons
                         |
               Relay of actions take place through the synapses
                         |
               New thought or idea perceived
                    (at the individual level)
```

Figure 5 . Human learning and memorisation process.

In other words a skill can be learnt and the mind improved with practice. In fact repetition improves the process of learning because it creates several pathways in the neural network of the brain which coordinate with each other [209]. In this way memory becomes stronger through the process of learning [210]. Although the whole learning process starts in the same fashion for all individuals it can reach different levels in different individuals. So even though anatomically all humans are the same, we can differ significantly depending on our learning aptitude and attitude. A person's intellect will in turn affect their perception and hence their opinions, further shaping their individualism. In other words, learning affects our perception, which, depending on what we learn and our ability to learn, will in turn result in differences of opinion.

The differences in the thought paths between individuals can be expressed as shown in Figure 6. Let us assume that two individuals, 'A' and 'B', have perceived the same new idea or thought. But in

Identity Through Science, Philosophy and Artistic Concepts in the Quran

processing that thought there is first a physiological difference in the DNA or genetic material (given as **1** and **2** in Figure 6) of individuals 'A' and 'B'. This difference in both nature and nurture will result in differences in the mechanisms of their thought processes (**3** and **4** in Figure 6). Therefore the individuals 'A' and 'B' may express a different opinion and/or emotion although they perceived the same idea or thought (**5** and **6** in Figure 6) [211] [212]. Therefore, the Quranic messages **'different background'** (30.22; 2.213; 10.19) and **'some are the same and some different'** (6.99, 100) can be described in both a philosophical and a scientific way.

BEGINNING OF THE PROCESS: Different individuals 'A' and 'B' perceive the 'same new thought'.
(Individuals of different background)

Path of thought

(1) DNA of "A"　　　　　(2) DNA of "B"

Different histone chemicals　　　Different histone chemicals

Character of "A" type mind　　　Character of "B" type mind

(3) 'A' type　←— thought processes —→　(4) 'B' type

"A"　←— two different people —→　"B"

(5) "A" type opinion　　　　(6) "B" type opinion

Difference in opinion
End of the process

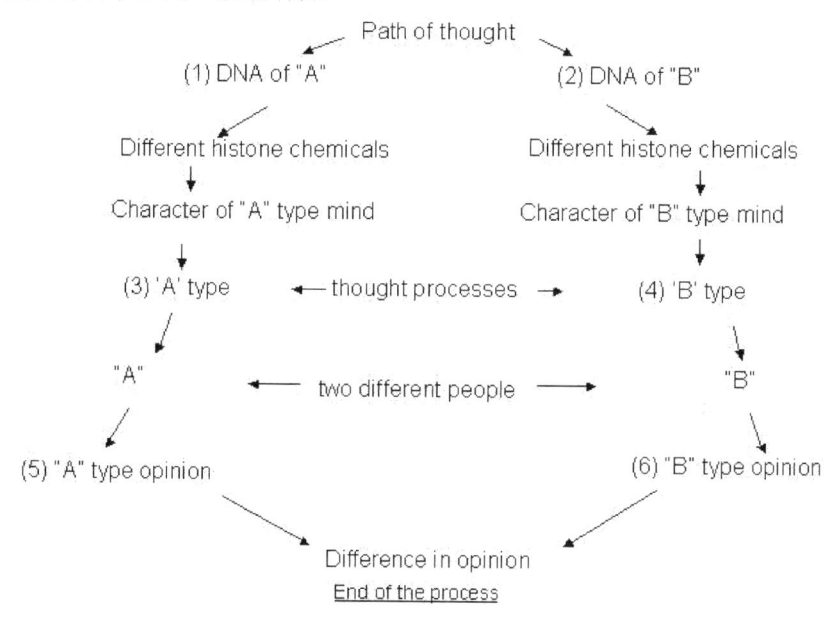

Figure 6. Difference in thought paths between individuals A and B.

Furthermore, an individual, e.g. 'A', may try to improve his or her understanding by repeating the thought and by understanding the process until the idea becomes clearer and rationalized. Whereas another individual, e.g. 'B', may not try very hard to understand and analyse the idea, and instead will accept it at face value, following its literal meaning.

So ultimately the thought process, perception and rationalization of ideas have led to very different expressions in two individuals, 'A' and 'B' [213], and shown differences in their attitude to learning. However, there may be other differences between persons 'A' and 'B', not been discussed here, that will influence their characteristics.

ECONOMIC AND CULTURAL DIFFERENCES

Wealth plays an important role in human life, enabling various social groups to behave differently depending upon their economic potential. In fact, within a community economic and cultural growth go hand in hand, and moral education may flourish only in communities that are not economically deprived. Economic stability and self-sufficiency obviously enable the development of a stable lifestyle and generate an independent mind. Similarly, a culture of patience and tolerance towards other people's points of view develops only where there is growth of knowledge and faith. The geographical background of any group or community also influences the development of their culture. However, as economy and culture are not directly relevant to the theme in this book, there will be no further discussions on these topics.

The author believes that Quranic wisdom helps to define the differences between two individuals, including the differences in their physical and intellectual conditions. These differences are generally recognized and accepted in the twenty-first century, but how do these differences influence the practise of Quranic philosophies?

PHILOSOPHY AND VARIABILITY

Firstly, what is philosophy and how can it influence the expression of emotion in human beings? Philosophy, or rationalism, is a system that studies the basic truth and principles of the universe, life and morals. It values differences and has been practised by many civilizations throughout history.

The author believes that the discourse between science and religion can be mediated by philosophy. Philosophy helps to distinguish between the natural sciences, social science and humanities. Similarly, it generates the need for greater understanding of life and human morals. An interdisciplinary approach to understanding each other may increase human awareness of the variability in our philosophies.

THE HANDLING OF HUMAN EMOTION

It is believed that philosophy plays a role in linking our mind to the rest of the world. Now, a basic philosophical premise is that if we understand something then we know it. For example, we know that eating healthy food is an important factor in our learning process [214]. When we see or smell delicious food our mind imagines how good the food will taste, which in turn stimulates our sensory organs and helps us to take the necessary steps towards eating the food. Here, food becomes food for thought. The philosophy behind this act is that our conscious psyche stimulates the body to take action as soon as we understand that the object is going to be beneficial to us. In contrast, if the mind does not consciously think that the food is beneficial then it could suppress the feeling of hunger.

The conscious mind can differentiate between a good and a bad action, or a right and a wrong thought. But only a free-thinking mind which is not constantly burdened by other factors, including economics and politics, will easily follow the morally correct path. In this instance we are discussing a phase or a state of mind which is better understood by scientists who study neuroscience [215] [216]. Neuroscience mainly deals with that part of the brain which is related to thought processes produced by nerves connected via neural networks. The latest discovery in this field is of a special type of brain cell that make humans different from other large animals [217]. Nowadays scientists have also discovered 'memes' or the building blocks of thought in humans, which constantly merge together or break up to produce ideas [218]. Therefore, with a free-thinking mind, a person is able to understand and produce ideas and judge situations wholeheartedly.

The brain's awareness comes from the *conscious* area, while the *unconscious* part of the brain is integral to the functioning of the whole structure. In fact, the greater part of the brain's task force constitutes the unconscious part of the mind, whereas only a small part represents conscious thought. Thus a large portion of the brain's activity occurs without our knowledge and remains beyond our control [219] [220] [221] [222].

The way the human mind reacts to an external signal can be roughly outlined as follows:

- the human eye sees something ...
- the signal goes to the unconscious brain ...
- the relevant processes trigger the conscious brain ...
- our subjective awareness of that object is raised.

Studies show that our brain produces the consciousness and its subjective state [223]. On the other hand, a computer can conduct a written conversation but it will not have any subjective awareness of what it is doing [224]. Through consciousness the human brain produces a series of emotions that lead us to such primal feelings as hunger, fear and anger. These feelings are the source of human values and self-esteem, and ultimately characterize us as individuals.

The rating of an individual as a good or a bad person is often dependent on their emotional state, as are his or her connections to other individuals [225]. Neuroscience has revealed that the unconscious part of the brain controls our free will and our decision-making process. Importantly, free will helps in the choice or determination of solutions [226]. In order to differentiate between the issues of morality and making conscious decisions three different situations have been described below:

- Me + computer = conversation (I ask to see something legal)
- A dialogue occurs and produces the situation of (a)
- I switch off the computer and the dialogue stops.

- Me + computer = conversation (I ask to see something illegal)
- A dialogue occurs and produces the situation of (b)
- I switch off the computer and the dialogue stops.
- Me + friend, we meet = conversation (I ask to see something illegal)
- A dialogue occurs and produces the situation of (c)
- My friend walks away as it is illegal.

The three situations described above have been labelled as (a), (b) and (c). In situation (a) the computer is having a virtual dialogue with me and obeying my command; in situation (b) the computer, i.e. a machine without any conscience, is obeying my order without asking the moral value of viewing something illegal; in situation (c), the human mind of my friend is conscious and has a conscience, and its subjective state asks the moral question of whether my suggestion is good or bad and responds accordingly. Human brainwaves help us to think and make important contributions when making conscious decisions [227]. The result of each situation will affect us and our self-esteem differently and any moral questioning will produce different emotional states within us.

Therefore, it can be said that philosophy determines a person's attitude towards his or her life. Although our individual philosophy may or may not be the same, we all want a minimum moral standard in our society [228]. In order to create a greater global understanding through an interdisciplinary approach, we need to exercise an approach to morality and discipline in common with other communities. In other words, each one of us needs to attain a wider perspective of life and morality.

'bestowed with limited freedom of thought – choice and action
(36.58–68; 17.84)

Human power and scientific knowledge both have their limits, and it is beyond our capacity to understand or claim to have full knowledge of the human mind or the universe. Many believe that the idea of absolute free will in a society is probably unrealistic and will ultimately bring about indiscipline and chaos. Since we are not always in full control of our emotions, the author feels that maintaining a basic moral standard in society is beneficial [229] [230].

THE CONTROLLING OF OLD AND MODERN URGES

The question that now arises is how and where do we draw the line when faced with our basic needs? Of course, opinions may vary because as individuals our perceptions of right and wrong are different and we judge according to our knowledge. The Prophet advised his followers to travel to China, if that was what was necessary to acquire knowledge. Following this tradition, the author has borrowed the verse below from the philosophies of 'Tao', which became popular in China almost 2,500 years ago:

'If you don't have enough to eat, work on getting enough to eat.

If you can't keep warm in winter, work on getting sufficient clothing.

If you don't have time to enjoy yourself, work toward getting leisure time.

But when you have had enough, you should stop.' [231]

This saying is still relevant today. It teaches us that we need to judge when we have adequately fulfilled our basic needs, such as eating or staying warm, and then stop using additional (natural) resources. However, perception of what is adequate varies from person to person.

Similarly, a modern philosopher, Mary Midgley (2001), has argued that good science is a good metaphor [232], implying that occasionally the goodness in science will need to be imposed rather than followed voluntarily by man. F. David Peat's (2006) theory on the 'saving of planet Gaia' points to a comparable view [233]. His theory concerns the irreversible environmental damage arising from our materialistic lifestyles and the resulting need to become conscious of the earth's future. Ideally, man should become more concerned about planet earth and its desecration [234]. The author believes that to portray the good side of human nature we need to show activities in which humane qualities or knowledge with piety will play a role. All branches of science, philosophy and religion need to work together towards this end [235] [236], and, as Prophet Muhammad (S:) said, 'seek that knowledge which is of benefit to humanity' [see ref. 135].

The next question to arise is what is the true human nature? Should we or should we not approve of dissimilarities between us?

THE TRUE HUMAN NATURE

'some believe, some do not' (18.29)
'human heart, eyes and ears fail to grasp the truth' (23.70, 71)

Through these verses the Quran portrays the differences in human understanding and belief. Moreover, it implies that the truth we seek may not be easy to find.

Most methodologies approved for research in the philosophy of science have a mathematical base. We also know that mathematics has been used as a tool to understand scientific observations and to model a variety of hypotheses. So it belongs to both philosophy and science. However, scientists and philosophers agree that there will always be some unknown or undiscovered areas, while mathematicians believe that some things cannot be calculated and are infinite [237].

This highlights the fact that an unknown nature exists and that this is currently beyond human assessment or comprehension. Several renowned scientists have expressed their views on the ultimately mysterious and unknown boundary of knowledge. The great philosopher and scientist Albert Einstein said: 'the fairest thing that we can experience is the mysterious' [238]. On another occasion he said: 'it takes the term of rapturous amazement at the harmony of natural law' [239]. In the same way Stephen Hawking, the famous cosmologist, believes that the mind of God may stay hidden for ever [240] [241]. Similarly, the celebrated naturalist David Attenborough admits that one must go on trying to understand the systems of nature, many of which are still unknown [242].

Today, the followers of science, philosophy and mathematics could well ask whether we may ever arrive at a stage where the ultimate boundaries in these subjects have been reached. Perhaps the human mind is at last accepting that although we are constantly moving forward, there seems to be no end in sight to the field of knowledge. As a result, dialogues have started between subjects such as religion and philosophy.

At the same time humans have not given up their search for the unknown and some are exploring the question 'how can we have a perfect understanding of the unknown?' In the search for knowledge two different schools of thought have emerged – those who feel that they have found the 'right direction' for ultimate knowledge and those who feel that 'the final direction is yet to be found'. Here the Quranic verse **'some believe, some do not'** (18.29) can be applied. That is to say, one group has considered the moral value of limitless pursuit and accepted the unknown gracefully, whereas the other group shows an inability to accept the limitlessness of their pursuit. However, the question remains as to whether future generations will understand or accept this notion.

THE FAILURE TO UNDERSTAND

Although today's children will build tomorrow's society, the current education system does not seem to have the facilities to encourage spiritual and moral teachings [243]; it is seen to be failing the spiritual test [244] [245]. Young minds need to learn social manners and to acknowledge as well as to appreciate others, but this concept seems to be missing from the education system. To give thanks to parents, teachers and God, for those who are believers, is not only good teaching but also inculcates good manners and creates a gentle and modest person. Of course, children need to be taught similar values at home as well.

Children in today's society face competition, failure and rejection, just like adults. As a result of feeling dejected and alienated, they soon learn how to take advantage of situations pitting the strong against the weak, just as adults do. One of the consequences is that juvenile crime has been on the increase. A local newspaper report stated that the police were asking parents to help tackle and reduce juvenile crime and antisocial behaviour [246]. Reports like this often lead us to conclude that perhaps teaching some aspects of morality both at home and at school might be of benefit. This is especially true as children often grow up in a self-centred and confusing world with little idea of how to choose between right and wrong. Moreover, they may not always be taught how to cope adequately with other points of view or with the diversities in life. Eventually this leads to a gap in understanding between adults and children, with adults often not perceiving that the gap is continually widening in the child's mind. Ultimately, the situation gets out of control, and by the time it comes to the attention of the parents, school, social workers or the criminal justice system it may be too late to save that particular child.

Just as morality or the moral intuition can influence our behaviour [247], moral teachings within peaceful philosophies can create an atmosphere of tolerance and adaptation in both the young and the old.

It is widely believed that competitive marketing is also making our society very consumerist. Words like moral, eternal peace and God play a small role in society's conscience. Although modern ideas and technologies may in future produce more beautiful, intelligent and healthier people [248], it will be a society without the freedom of *contentment*. For instance, it is popular for families and friends to go on holiday to unwind; but if there is a dearth of peace in their daily lives then a package tour for a limited period of time might not provide happiness for the rest of the year.

In the end the selfishness in human nature seems to overpower human piety. We forget that happiness is not available in the supermarket, but that it is inside our mind. Contentment of the mind is a mirage in today's consumer society, which drowns true happiness through various temporary and superficial satisfactions. The failure of today's society to rectify the gap between a contented and a discontented mind seems to have led to many of the ills, injustices and sufferings that are common worldwide.

In other words there remains a big gap in understanding the difference between pleasure and contentment within today's social infrastructure. Many people pass through life in an unhappy and frustrated state, with competitiveness being the mantra of normal life. Corporate status rather than inner peace seems to be the trademark of the modern world, with the media playing a large role in advocating who has achieved the top position.

Old and young both endure aggressive pressure from extreme competitiveness, with some unable to cope with the pressure and succumbing to depression, committing suicide or performing homicide. The latter individuals seem unable to find a peaceful acceptance of social norms. As a result society has become a two-tiered structure in which one group marches on successfully while the other gets crushed silently. Perhaps it does not help that, although through modern science a brain scan is able to detect our brain structure, we are not yet able to ascertain our moral nature [249].

We next discuss the question of where and what is today's philosophy.

TRUSTFUL BELIEFS

What is the ultimate philosophy of life?

To many people the ultimate aim in life is to be happy. But what is happiness? Happiness can be many things. However, a long-lasting happiness can occur from a lack of anxiety, because that brings us peace. Although in practice peace might be a temporary phase of mind, a more permanent condition might be faith, because it generally leads to a feeling of contentment. This view is supported by scientific research [250; see also ref. 79]. We can accept the idea of faith only when we are ready to accept the constituent parts of that faith. Once our mind starts to feel content it begins to trust the event that led to that state. Many religious beliefs have gradually developed this trust through practice.

In some religious traditions, freeing the mind from the stresses of worldly affairs is taken as the final phase in being liberated and finding peace. In most faiths, the feeling of being liberated is thought to come through devotional practice. For instance, in Buddhism, meditation is advised for liberating the mind and the soul of the individual [251] [252]. In this faith the main aim is to liberate the mind from worldly pressures. Buddhists believe that the liberated mind is peaceful in the mortal life and it makes the individual happy.

FAITHFUL PHILOSOPHIES

We need to ask the question: what is faith?

The author believes that it is complete trust or confidence in some ultimate power. This is a state of mind where the individual feels that he or she is performing a most dutiful and holy task, and becomes a *believer*. The performance of acts of faith may, however, vary from religion to religion. In contrast, science believes in actions based on logic and does not follow a philosophy or belief out of devotion. Nonetheless, strict rules and procedures are followed by modern scientists, similar to those in religious practices, where *moral codes and disciplines* in life are followed through a sense of *duty and responsibility*. The Quranic message of **'some are the same and some different'** (6.99, 100) can also be applied to differences in philosophical thought and faith.

Is it only prayers and rituals that bind a mind to a religion? Are there any other reasons why people are attracted towards devotion? Now, science has helped us to explain and advance our knowledge of life. Why, then, would an intelligent mind seek wisdom beyond science (such as in religious studies)? The answer lies in the fact that to date science has used innovative knowledge to provide answers to a wide range of problems (for example, science can show us pictures of distant stars), but it has yet to discover a formula for creating happiness, peace or ever-lasting contentment.

The author's research on faith revealed that in the book *Watching the English* sociologist Kate Fox claimed that only 18 per cent of the British population, including Muslims, Christians and Jews, answered the statement 'I am a practising member of an organized religion' positively [253]. Of course, it can be said that a person may not be a practising individual but may still have a particular kind of *belief*. It is thought that believers have an inclination to seek the help, guidance and companionship of God because the perception of an ever-living presence in this temporary and makeshift world is comforting and gives reassurance. For believers, prayer involves the soul's effort to reach out towards the ultimate and infinite power, which is attributed to God. This bonding can become firm and permanent, providing assurance during calamity and distress.

Perhaps this feeling deep inside the mind of the believer can be called faith.

Some part of our existence is related to the body, whilst other parts are related to the mind. A number of people have argued that the mind can extend beyond the brain [254]. This is true in certain contexts, such as imagination, which extends beyond the physical boundaries of the brain. On the other hand, according to popular belief, the soul relates to both the physical life of the mortal world and the eternal life that is beyond this world.

Maybe we can now accept the soul as the province of contentment.

EVERLASTING CONTENTMENT

Everlasting contentment needs to encompass the human body, mind and soul, i.e. man's total existence. However, what is the soul? The soul has been defined in dictionaries in a variety of ways:

1. The spiritual or immaterial part of an individual.
2. A person's spiritual or immortal element.
3. The spiritual and immortal part of human beings.

Identity Through Science, Philosophy and Artistic Concepts in the Quran

4. The seat of human personality, intellect, will and emotions – i.e. an entity that survives death.

5. The non-physical aspect of a person – i.e. a spirit surviving death. [255; 256; 257; 258; 259]

However, we are yet to discover or explain where the seat or the basis of the soul is in the human body. Various cultures describe the soul in different ways, although a closer study will reveal a common theme. A number of definitions of the soul from different cultures and religions are given below:

1. Amerindian
   a) 'Free soul' departs the body at death;
   b) 'Breath soul'/'Life'.

2. Ancient Egyptian
   a) The 'Ba' or 'Soul';
   b) The 'Ka' or 'Spirit' for after-death life.

3. Australian Aborigines
   a) 'Human and immortal soul' from parents;
   b) 'Immortal and eternal soul', which comes from and returns to totemic ancestors.

4. Zorastrianism
   a) 'Fravashi'/man's eternal spirit, which remains in heaven;
   b) Even during his life on earth.

5. Hinduism
   'Atman' – 'Breath' or 'principle of life'.

6. Judaism — 'Soul' – immortal, is rewarded or punished by God.

7. Christianity — Soul survives death:
   a) Catholicism (Roman) – saved souls undergo a period of purification;
   b) Protestantism – a few enter the immediate presence of God.

8. Islamic — 'Ruh'/Soul/Spirit – the permanent 'individuality' of man, which is immortal [260; 261; 262; 263; 264; 265; 266; 267; 268; 269; 270].

These descriptions show that it seems acceptable across religions and cultures to believe that the end of the physical form of life is not the final form of the spirit, which can continue thereafter in another form. In the three monotheistic religions the soul has only one track, which continues from this life to eternity. Definition of the soul given above also shows that in most faiths the human soul is associated with the positive, whether it be liberty or peace, or submission to a devotional source.

It is interesting to note that Islam describes the soul as having a permanent human individuality, which gives importance not only to our mortal life but also that after death. Since one of the goals that humans aim for is recognition, and according to Islam all our good and bad deeds are imprinted on our soul, we can say that Islam recognizes human actions throughout their lives. In other words, our actions become part of our souls and help to develop our individuality. According to the monotheistic faiths, including Islam, it is believed that a human can achieve complete individualism only when his or her physical self, as well as his or her mind and soul, travel together along the *good* track of life with *good* intentions and *good* actions. Monotheistic beliefs insist that in the afterlife the individual will follow the outcomes of the actions and intentions resulting from his or her mortal life, which have resulted in a *good* or a *bad* soul. It is believed in Islam that the status of the soul cannot be changed once a person has died.

Connecting with worldly affairs and being true to the supreme power is a practice of good deed found in every faith. To elaborate, one has only to look deep inside the believer's mind and, regardless of their faith, understand their primary act of devotion. At this stage of worship, communicating with God remains the ultimate goal of an individual because sharing the burdens of life and trying to find solace often bring relief and contentment for that person. The author believes that mortal life is a continuous process and that its continuity in a peaceful manner is the ultimate good deed in life.

MIND/SOUL - A PLACE FOR PEACE?

Mankind has regularly asked whether peace comes with spiritual nearness to God. If we accept that the soul exists within the human mind, then can we assert that the human soul or mind yearns for peace at the deepest level?

In modern times many religious philosophies have been discarded as 'old ideas from the past' that are not compatible with the new technological era. We are told that all future advancement and functioning of society will be controlled by computerized and televised technology, which would revolutionize all aspects of education and access to knowledge. Even today the world is learning about life and accessing knowledge, whether old or new, through the internet. In our era of rapid growth of knowledge it is sometimes easy to forget that all we have achieved today is based upon yesterday's learning.

We now accept that the human mind is founded on the model of the human body [271], and that is how modern neurosurgery and modern philosophy assume our body–mind (soul) relationship works. Scientists have found other ways to explain the relationship between the human body and mind, including through the use of religion. Albert Einstein admitted that the Greek philosopher Spinoza had influenced his religious thoughts and in 'The World as I See It' he explained his feelings as religiousness of science [272].

Mark Forstater's article on 'The Meditations of Marcus Aurelius's *Cultivating the Self* discusses this subject well [273]. It summarizes ideas from the ancient philosopher on ways to control our willpower, and perhaps find peace, through: (1) moral cultivation, (2) pleasure of wisdom, (3) reason and virtue, (4) nurturing the truth, (5) survival by simplicity, (6) no time to waste, (7) action and intention, (8) concentration of the ruling mind, (9) no regret, (10) limiting judgement and (11) self-control.

As mentioned earlier, we do not always remember that our current wisdom stands on the shoulders of historical experiences. Some people may feel that history relates to *old* ideas, but others may ask how time can become *old* when it is always moving forward [274]. In our minds we conceptualize ideas differently from each other; for example, some people may not believe that there is a Creator of time, space and knowledge, whereas others do. Could we call this difference in belief an expression of diversity of thought? Only once we have accepted such differences can we accept the true diversity in the nature of the Creator, who has created these differences within humans. The author believes that in this way we might possibly capture an elusive peace of mind.

UNITY AND DIVERSITY IN HUMAN FAITH AND PHILOSOPHIES

This section cites examples relating to unity and diversity in humans according to different British communities and faiths:

Bhagavata Purana   Hinduism
'The Lord creates, preserves and reabsorbs the universe – the power of the Lord is infinite – though He is the maker of this world he remains forever beyond it (choose submission).' [275]

Adi Granth   Sikhism
'The nature of God is Absolute, formless – power overawed the entire world.'[276]

<u>Meditation</u>   Buddhism

'Open your mind

Broaden your horizon

Try to trace the source of the problem.' [277]

<u>Community Healing</u>   Christianity

'All power is from God, so that every observed phenomenon of nature and every moment of history exists only because He supports and sustains it.'   [278]

In the twentieth century Mother Teresa of Kolkata set a new tradition in prayers for the Christian community. Her prayers not only include charitable love for mankind at large but also services to bring peace in society:

> 'The fruit of silence is prayer
> The fruit of prayer is faith
> The fruit of love is service
> The fruit of service is peace.' [279]

A similar idea is seen in the Shaker community:

'God is the Giver of all good, and we are His servants, who in various ways, have received abilities that will fit us for the duties of life which we are to perform, and it should be our highest aim to make a wise and prudent use of all the faculties with which we are endowed.' [280]

The Jewish rabbi Lionel Blue has said:

> '"Thou shalt understand thyself" –
> All that I am
> All that I do
> All that I will ever have
> I offer now to you.

All that I dream
All that I pray
All that I ever make
I give you today.' [281]

Muslim Sufis have left a vast collection of stories on the relationship between different communities and the relationship of the human soul with God. These stories can also be taken as teachings for us to follow.

This story from the Sufis is composed of a variety of natural phenomena, namely *stream, wind, voice, sand, mountain* and *rain*. Here, human nature is represented through *stream*, as it brings life; wisdom or nature's forward knowledge is represented as the *wind*, which is forever moving forward; the *voice* represents the inspirational power for good present within all living beings; *sand* represents the stagnant state where anything new is prohibited and all living things dry up; the *mountain* represents hardship in the path of achievement and *rain* on the ground represents blessing for new life.

'The *Wind* is crossing the desert, the *stream* is told by the whispering voice,

The *stream* wanted to understand more

The *voice* tells the *stream* to be carried by the *wind*

The *stream* is nervous to take the first step

But on the *voice's* insistence the stream stretches its arms to the *wind* and is carried away

The *voice* warns that if the *stream* does not venture to the new, it would dry up in the *sands*. The *stream* turns into vapour and is carried many miles before it dashes against the *mountain* and dropped as *rain* on the ground.' [282]

The above transliterated verses from stories told by Sufis can be interpreted as follows. At first humans were hesitant to take unknown steps into the future but they were persuaded through inspiration from God and belief that His help was near by. Thus the essential nature of human endeavour, which was hidden under ignorance, was tested; inspiration then allowed humans to venture into new spheres through hardship.

One common theme emerges from these collections of faith-based and philosophical ideas, which is liberation of the human soul, whether by submission to God or by broadening the human horizon. It now becomes clear how the human mind unites and then divides in its philosophy of life according to religious or cultural background. We can therefore surmise that culture influences faith and vice versa.

The next question is: do the world's faithful unite in their beliefs?

UNITY IN THE MONOTHEISTIC FAITHS

A variety of tenets about the unity of God, and the preservation of monotheism, are found in the Holy Scriptures. These include:

- The Quran

  'No partner to Allah'
  'Do good to parents'
  'Do not kill [unless justified]'
  'Do justice [act with fairness]'
  (s.v 6.52)

- The Old Testament

  One God, no other God/gods
  Honour parents
  Do not murder
  Do not give false witness (Exod. 20.12)

- The New Testament

  There is only One who is good
  Respect your father and your mother

Do not commit murder

Do not accuse falsely (Matt. 19.17–19)

The above quotations show that in the monotheistic belief of 'One God' the preservation of His human society remains the key to a successful community. Therefore, those who are faithful within monotheism seem to have the same belief and yet are diverse in their practices within our society.

RECENT ACTS OF UNITY IN MAN

Human and other lives can encounter calamities of an extraordinary scale, such as hurricanes, tsunamis, droughts, avalanches or disasters of a similar nature. During such turbulent times faith in God, which can remain buried deep inside us, often emerges. For example, during the Hillsborough football disaster, some of the panicked spectators started to pray [283]. It is common for a sense within us to guide us in those dark moments to be humble and to seek assurance in a greater power. The tsunami in the Indian Ocean on 26 December 2004 also showed how numerous people who had lost all hope turned to prayers. In these circumstances people were at a loss, but instead of blaming God they assembled to pray together for eternal peace and solidarity in this life.

In the next section the author has cited verses from three suras, 'The Philosophy of Quranic Unity', 'Prayer for Guidance' and 'True Believer', to explain how the Quran points out that besides true believers there will always be those who do not believe. True believers will follow their conscience with purity, abide by social and natural laws to coexist with other creations and attempt to create a peaceful life in this world.

Identity Through Science, Philosophy and Artistic Concepts in the Quran

The Philosophy of Quranic Unity

'God! There is no God but Him, the Living, the Eternal One. Neither slumber nor sleep overtakes Him. His is what the heavens and the earth contain. Who can intercede with Him except by His permission?
He knows what is before and behind man. They can grasp only the part of His knowledge which He wills. His throne is as vast as the heavens and the earth, and the preservation of both does not weary Him. He is the Exalted, the Immense One.'
(2.255)

The above Quranic verses portray the unity of God, and their description of 'The Absolute and Supreme Fundamental Source of Power' is the central belief in Islam. Teachings from this philosophy guide mankind towards the important notion that we can find support and gain confidence from God.

Prayer for Guidance

'Praise be to God, Lord of the Universe,
The Compassionate the Merciful,
Sovereign of the Day of Judgement
You alone we worship, and to you alone we turn for help
Guide us to the straight path
The path of those whom You have favoured,
Not of those who have incurred your wrath,
Nor of those who have gone astray.' (1.1–7)

These verses suggest that man should approach God humbly and ask Him for guidance.

True Believer

If we were to ask the question how can a person become a true believer, then we would find certain advice in the Quran:

'of all His servants, only such as are endowed with knowledge stand truly in awe of God' (112.1–4)
'the truth is from God, some believe and some not' (18.29)
'purity, harmony and law drive away evil' (30.3)

According to the Quran, only a few knowledgeable people understand and wonder at the nature of God's eternal power and His infinite creativity, and only a few prefer His company and believe in His guidance.

MANKIND IN THE QURAN AND DIVERSITY AMONGST THE FAITHFULS

'mankind was one single nation, but [became] **different later'** (10.19)
'created different languages, colours and nationalities' (2.213)

These verses explain that individualism exists within man, and should be accepted as such. They suggest that in prehistoric times human beings were initially unified as a single community or nation, but as we evolved into many communities and nations the name mankind became more suitable. Humans show diversity in their physical and mental characteristics, whether influenced by genetics or the environment, as well as across cultural, geographical and economic backgrounds. The Quran is exact in its description of human diversity as **'languages, colours and nationalities'** (2.213).

Currently, the Muslim community is seen as being universally fragmented, especially in the British Isles [284]. The author believes that a brief understanding of the background of Muslims in today's Britain is appropriate at this stage. Although approximately 69 per cent of British Muslims are from the Indian subcontinent [285], Arabs, Iranians and various other nationalities also contribute to the total, while Muslim communities from eastern Europe and parts of Africa are recent migrants to the UK. Despite differences in geographic and cultural backgrounds, most Muslims in Great Britain adhere to the principles of Islam, persevering in the observance and conviction of their religious duties, i.e. following one God and accepting Prophet Muhammad (S:) as His messenger.

Quranic messages encourage Muslims to have tolerance and treat members of both Muslim and non-Muslim communities with respect, since variety and differences in human nature were both created by God.

Hajj, or the annual obligatory pilgrimage, which should be performed at least once in the lifetime of a Muslim, is an occasion where the idea of unity and diversity is implemented through millions of pilgrims bound together in brotherly acts. Here everyone accepts their own cultural and national differences, but performs the obligatory spiritual act, cooperating in every possible way and reciting the same prayers to God. Prophet Muhammad

(S:) performed the first Hajj when he visited Makkah from Medina before his death in AD 632. The prayer is:

> 'I am, here I am
> Thou have no associate.
> Thine is all Praise,
> All Grace,
> And all horizon
> Thou have no associate.'

In this prayer the Prophet Muhammad (S:) praises all the beneficial and useful things which have been bestowed upon mankind, and on the whole living universe, as God's grace. He also acknowledges that diversity exists amongst mankind and in creation, thus verifying God's grace across *all horizons*. The prayer shows the Prophet's understanding of Islamic philosophy through his proclamation of and submission to God's absolute and unquestionable supremacy. By reciting this prayer during Hajj, Muslims show their acceptance of God's grace *across all horizons*, and that of diversity in individuals.

The criteria we use to identify the concept of 'self' start at the beginning of our life and define and accentuate the boundary between *us* and *them*. These self-imposed criteria are tested to their limit during the course of our lifetime, especially when building relationships with others, because we have to acknowledge and accept that there are differences between individuals. This perception of difference is integral to our ability to identify and recognize self as an individual, which is distinct from others.

The author believes that the words 'perfect' or 'right', in absolute terms, are not applicable to mankind, which goes through various emotional stages at different times of life. At most, a person can identify that he or she has certain characteristics that allow them to be self-assured and confident.

Conclusion

In this discussion about the Quranic concept of unity and diversity in humans the author has explored biological, philosophical and spiritual aspects of our personalities using philosophy and science. We can say that to understand the philosophy of unity and diversity which binds our pan-human society we need to understand the identity of individuals who together form society. Differences in chemical composition at the body's molecular level, people's attitude to learning, their philosophical aims in life, as well as their socio-economic and geographic background, help to establish different human personalities in communities. We expect individuals to control their expressions of morality and selfishness, while their determination and perseverance can help modify society. Finally, most major religions, in particular Islam, believe that God has intended or ordered harmonious existence despite the natural presence of diversity. Humans often ignore this reality, although, the author believes, it should be at the forefront of their consciousness in relation to their own identity and that of others.

The question remains whether human fulfilment can be sought in any other way other than through philosophy and morality?

Chapter Five

FULFILMENT: CREATIVE ART

REALIZATION

'**all things good, beautiful and useful are from God**'
(10.2; 59.22–24)
'[the] **preservation of heaven and earth does not weary Him**'
(2.255; 42.49–50)

The above verses indicate that the creation of an artistic God results in '**good, beautiful and useful**' things and that the '**preservation**' of this art '**does not weary Him**'. Since the universe is thought to be an ingenious process of creation filled with originality in every aspect of life, we could consider it to be an ongoing artistic process produced by God. The word beautiful has many connotations, including form, shape, idea, rhythm, colour, style, sound, music, poetry, storytelling and the juxtaposition of words. In essence beauty can be found in whatever a mind can see or imagine or perceive, and even in matters beyond human perception.

The author believes that fulfilment comes from within us when our achievements or accomplishments are met with gratification and satisfaction. Whether beauty can help in this process remains the final point in this discussion on human identity. In order to understand fulfilment we need to question whether the concept of beauty can be found at the deepest level beyond the boundaries of comprehension.

The day the first human consciously picked up a flower and looked at its beauty with awe and smelled its fragrance with wonder was probably the dawn of the appreciation of beauty; and possibly, when humans first looked up at the beautiful colours of a twilight sky and felt humble their devotional or spiritual feelings were born. Awe and wonder are two human emotions which are generally associated with beauty and often linked to art. A piece of art can be expressed in colour, in sound, in structure, in words, or even in the manner in which a story is told. Art can also be described using expressions such as creative, original and ingenious. Generally, art starts as an idea or imagining that gradually takes shape to become the artist's final product – be it as a colour, shape or concept. In other words, the artist's goal is to make the audience feel, see, listen to and appreciate the artistic endeavour. Fortunately, the human brain is adept at spotting artistic beauty, pattern and style in both natural and man-made environments [286] [287].

THE ARTIST

'contemplate the wonders of creation' (3.191)
'the sole Creator, the Maker – the Shaper – the Fashioner' (28.12–14; 59.24)

Different translators of the above Quranic verses have used different adjectives, such as **'Maker – Shaper – Fashioner'**, to qualify God's artistic nature. Humans need to observe His creation and appreciate it with an open mind, and take God as a supreme artist or as the source of continuity in this ongoing universal process of *creative art*. However, according to the Quran this Creator of all artistic knowledge does not wait for our appreciation, neither does He need our approval. It is up to humans to look around with awe and wonder at the beauty that encompasses life in different colours and shapes across the natural world. Whether or not we appreciate these artistic phenomena, which influence our daily lives, is another matter.

THE ARTIST'S ART

'all things good, beautiful and useful are from God' (10.2; 59.22–24)

Usually the criterion for qualification as an artist is that there is an audience to appreciate the work of art [288]. If a piece of art reflects the true emotions of the artist, and the art has an extraordinarily expressive quality, then the artist is more likely to become successful. So if the Creator is the ultimate artist as **'all things good, beautiful and useful are from God'** (10.2; 59.22–24), then His Book, the Quran, also shares the glory of being a great piece of art. By admiring the exquisite art contained inside this divine Book, we can increase our limited ideas of God, the supreme artist.

'the Quran, recite and contemplate' (17.45–48)
'of all His servants, only such as are endowed with knowledge, stand truly in awe of God' (112.1–4)

The author believes that the evidence of God's creativity can be found in infinite ways across time, and that the revelations in the Quran are part of this wonder. Humans are asked to understand the Quran with **'awe'** (112.1–4) and **'contemplate'** (17.45–48) its meaning through enquiry and observation. In other words the idea of contemplation entails not only appreciating the meaning of Quranic verses through an enquiring mind but also remembering God with **'awe'** (112.1–4) and wondering at the intricate artistic ideas evolving through all natural phenomena in the universe.

Identity Through Science, Philosophy and Artistic Concepts in the Quran

ARTISTIC APPEAL

We know that scientific formulae and precision in methodology are required to produce an object or to prove an idea, whereas artistic patterns and feelings can produce a striking piece of art [289] [290]. The relationship between nature and the human mind can be explored through art, because the artistic media can express the artist's emotions and feelings, e.g. colours in a painting, type of music, etc. The created object or idea is then accepted by society as art. In this way both art and science, which are governed by certain rules, contribute to our store of knowledge. For instance, there is always a beginning and an end to a piece of creative work [291], just as there are boundaries associated with a scientific hypothesis. Since art is generally taken as something which appeals to the senses, e.g. sight, touch [292], the enjoyment of having observed and appreciated an artist's work may linger for a long time afterwards. Appreciation and enjoyment remain the main theme or appeal in a piece of artwork. Therefore, a visible and tangible form of art will continue to appeal as long as it survives through time.

In the context of the Quran as a piece of art, during different periods of time many authors have acknowledged that 'the variety in the language and style of the Quran' is strikingly forceful, beautiful and artistic [293]. Similarly, the Quran has been noted as a source of artistic inspiration and sublime enjoyment by many commentators [294] [295]. In this chapter we will examine the Quran as a piece of creative art that is appealing and continuously revitalizing humans as well as providing us with knowledge.

THE STYLE OF HISTORY AND IMAGINATION IN THE QURAN

Chronology or measuring objects or notions through time is indispensable, since without it there would be no categorization in history. We can also see a chronological sequence in the development of art. As we look at past experiences or events which make up history, we find that many historical records have been left through artistic sketches and drawings. A historical fact is displayed artistically when an individual's imagination records the shape of an image in the past and thereby commemorates it. Although, interestingly, such art is a creation of the past, it continues to exist in the present.

A work of art from a certain period of history also represents it as a function of that historical period. In other words, the work of art reproduces the past whether in words, colour or crafts to be admired at the present time [296] [297]. Looking at art through the ages, the author believes that the Quran fits the description of a work of art. It not only uses a number of styles but also narrates human events with historical allegory, explaining episodes chronologically through storytelling so that past events become realistic for the reader. In this way even today, whether in traditional cultures or otherwise, the art of storytelling both entertains and gives historical information [298] [299].

ARTISTIC TRUTH AND REALITY

Artistic truth is a literary theory [300]. Artistic truth helps art to interact with reality and thereby determines its social function [301]. The artistic technique that best reveals the truth about a specific event or fact is the one that will be accepted most readily by the viewer. Such an interpretation will portray reality according to the artist and stay in the mind of the viewer. The author believes that the Quran, the natural world and the human mind all display this artistic inclination. Therefore, to establish an interaction between art and reality, one has to trace where art embodies reality in the Quran and in nature, as well as in human creativity.

Our interest in art requires it to be considered in all its complexity and to take into account the fact that artistic truth manifests itself in different forms and through different methods. Artistic studies consider man as the subject of history [302], and through their human focus the artist or the writer can show us the mind-set of the people, place and events of a particular age. Sometimes the *typical character* to emerge from the core of a piece of art becomes the reference point that reveals the trueness of that period [303].

Identity Through Science, Philosophy and Artistic Concepts in the Quran

Using this analogy, we can assert that Prophet Muhammad (S:) is the *typical character* of the Quran. In other words, his character explains the nucleus of the Quran and portrays the energy of its principles. The beauty of the Quranic dialogues from the Creator to His creations is conveyed through Prophet Muhammad (S:), the Messenger. The Messenger's role is to present all knowledge within the created art form, in this case the Quran, to man, whilst the artist, the Creator, remains in the background.

Islam does not give credit to man for any shape, form, idea or event that he may have created. According to Islam, whether it be a divine scripture or art created by human hands, all scientific or artistic phenomena and expressions within the natural world are the work of God. In the Quran, nobody and nothing qualifies for the divine status of Almighty God the Creator; not even Prophet Muhammad (S:).

This is the fundamental point where Islam diverges from other theological or philosophical views, where many man-made objects of art created in various forms are considered to be divine. In such instances the human mind slowly develops an idea of veneration for many artistic manifestations, which in the end earn devotion from their devotees. In its simplest form this devotion sometimes attributes divinity to the object. The Quranic teaching of art carefully guides mankind and his piety towards the ultimate creative powers of God and away from the worshipping of His creations.

The natural world, however, remains an area where varieties, which we can take as examples of divine artistic expression, repeatedly unfold, whether seen or unseen by the human eye. In other words, although we are surrounded by many natural beauties, these are often taken for granted and some may even go unobserved in our lifetime.

NATURAL AND BEAUTIFUL

'all things good, beautiful and useful are from God'   (10.2; 59.24)

The author will now examine whether or not we can claim that our daily experiences are natural and beautiful.

If we extend our imagination beyond its immediate boundaries, then our conscious mind would perceive art in every aspect of our lives. According to Muslim Sufis, 'God reveals Himself by the very act of creation' (1997) [304]. They believe that any appreciation of beauty in the natural world allows our mind to feel the artistic touch of the Supreme Artist. Through the act of perceiving God's work it becomes a reality for humans, and thereby leads us to admire and wonder at the art in nature.

Whether it is a clear starry night or a green pasture under the blue sky or an infant smiling, not many of us can resist pausing and appreciating beauty. These scenes from our everyday life are natural and **'beautiful'**, and may also serve a **'good – useful'** purpose (10.2; 59.24). In this way we can understand the Sufi philosophy of God revealing himself through the natural world.

Whether we are observing the beauty in nature or man-made art, or listening to poetry or music, we often appreciate artists and their artwork more if they resemble something familiar or we can identify with them. So, besides beauty, the next quality in art that draws our attention is often, although not always, its familiar or realistic appearance. Some sources believe that artistic truth is life's truth aesthetically interpreted, and that it is part of human living [305] [306] [307]. If art produces a feeling of reality or is personalized then its appeal has credibility. According to modern mathematicians the human brain is wonderful at spotting patterns in nature and recognizing self [308], both of which are concepts that artists often portray in their art.

We can even argue that there is a hidden quality within us that is expressed only when touched by real beauty. Beauty is natural and settles well within the human persona, although the sentiment may need to be awakened. The perception of beauty may differ from one person to another, but in the end beauty can be appreciated by all. The author believes that artistic philosophy should touch the hearts and minds of all men and women.

THE ARTISTIC QURAN

This section will analyse the Quran's structure and narrative style through art. This will be followed by a discussion on the comparative beauty in nature and in man-made art as appreciated through the

Identity Through Science, Philosophy and Artistic Concepts in the Quran

Quranic verses. The discussion attempts to improve our understanding of the variety in the Supreme Artist's styles and artistic methods, which are revealed in the Quran and in His creation. This Quranic analysis should enhance our awareness of the inner beauty within us. Since art is appreciated by people to different levels at different times in their lives and in many different ways, such awareness cannot be mass produced.

The author addresses the above points in the next three sections of this chapter:

1. Art in the Holy Quran.
2. Art in Nature – the Quranic Concept.
3. Art Representing Mankind – the Quran's Influence.

1.
Art in the Holy Quran

This section will explore Quranic verses for 1) artistic structural concepts and 2) beautiful expressions which are realistic and natural and can be grouped together as creative art.

1)   Artistic Structural Concepts in the Quran

In this section verses from the Quran have been compiled to produce a structural model of the text and a graphic design of human development through the different stages of life.

   (i)   A Structural Model of the Holy Quran

The chronological sequence of events in the Quran and its appeal as a literary style were discussed earlier (see prelude chapter on the Quran). In the Quran, historical narrations are not like in the Bible but allegorical, and serve to describe people from seventh-century Arabia and surrounding countries. For centuries Muslims have tried to beautify Quranic pages and its writings with shiny colours and vivacious patterns. However, these artistic efforts have appeared from within the human imagination and may even distract from the beauty within the verses. These verses, the author advocates, can be of indescribable beauty and can be understood by those who want to explore their depths without the additional embellishment of man-made art. Interestingly, mathematics is thought to be helpful in appreciating the artistic wonders of the Quran, and various Muslims, including the author, have explored this view further.

As mentioned earlier, there are 114 chapters or suras in the Quran. The verses or ayas in each sura are arranged in a different order, with some suras having only a few verses whereas others have many. The author explored the organization of Quranic suras by grouping suras with the same number of verses together. This resulted in a distinct shape that can be considered as the inherent structural design of the Quran (see Figure 7). In other words, the composition of verses in the Quranic suras represents a pyramid structure. This formation is artistic in that it conveys succinctly a structural model of the Quran.

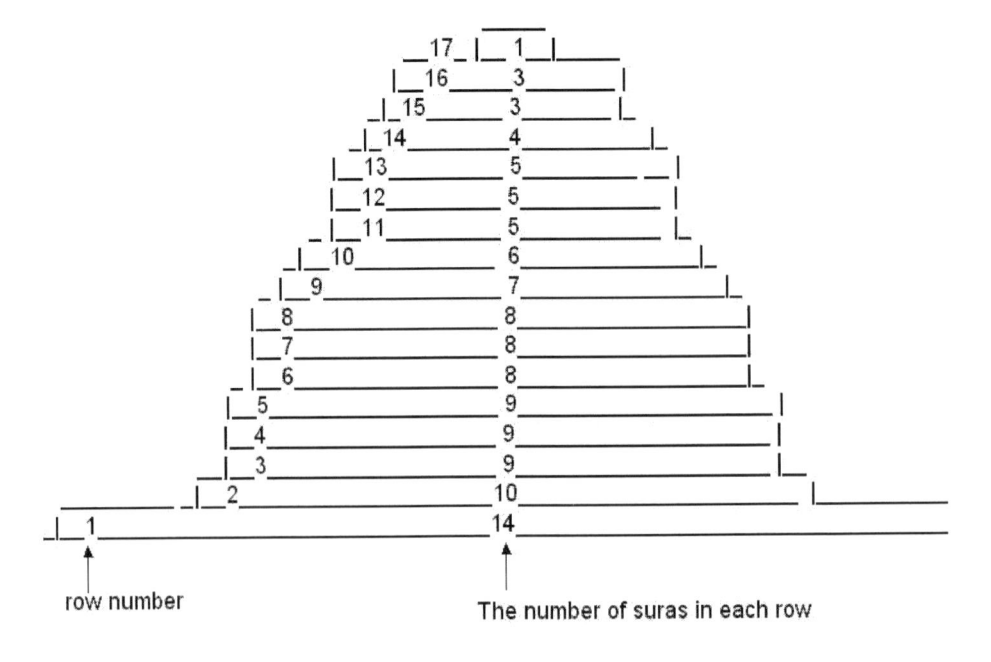

```
                    _17_|_ 1_|_
                   |__16____3_____|
                  _|_15_____3_____L_
                 _|_14_____4_____|_
                |__13_____5_____ _|
                |__12_____5_____|
               _|__11_____5_____L_
              _|__10_____6_____|_
             _|__9_____7_____L_
            |__8_____8_____|
            |__7_____8_____|
           _|__6_____8_____L_
          |__5_____9_____|
          |__4_____9_____|
         _|__3_____9_____L_
        _|__2_____10_____|_
_|__1_____14_____
     ↑                             ↑
  row number              The number of suras in each row
```

Fig. 7. A model of the structural design of the quranic text

Identity Through Science, Philosophy and Artistic Concepts in the Quran

In Figure 7, the seventeen rows each contain a certain number of suras. The suras in every row have a similar number of verses, e.g. row number seven contains eight suras with between twenty and twenty-six verses each. The pyramid shape gradually tapers as the number of suras decreases with the ascending number of verses contained within them. Suras that exemplify each row of the pyramid are given in Table 3.

Table 3. Key to the Quranic Composition Model

Row Number	Number of Suras in Each Row	Quranic Number for Suras Represented in Each Row	Verses in Each Sura
1	14	31, 32, 45, 46, 47, 48, 57, 67, 71, 72, 76, 81, 83, 89	28-38
2	10	14, 34, 41, 42, 52, 54, 68, 69, 74, 77	49-56
3	9	1, 94, 95, 99, 98, 102, 107, 109, 114	6-8
4	9	49, 60, 61, 64, 82, 86, 87, 91, 96	13-19
5	9	97, 103, 105, 106, 108, 110, 111, 112, 113	3-5
6	8	62, 63, 65, 66, 93, 100, 101, 104	9-12
7	8	58, 59, 73, 84, 85, 88, 90, 92	20-26
8	8	13, 35, 50, 70, 75, 78, 79, 80	40-46
9	7	8, 22, 25, 29, 33, 39, 55	69-78
10	6	5, 9, 11, 16, 20, 23	118-135
11	5	10, 12, 17, 18, 2	109-112
12	5	24, 30, 44, 51, 53	59-64
13	5	28, 36, 38, 40, 43	83-89
14	4	19, 15, 27, 56	93-99
15	3	4, 6, 37	165-182
16	3	7, 3, 26	200-227
17	1	2	286

Although the structural design (Figure 7) does not convey a philosophical idea, it shows an intrinsic artistic pattern within the Quran. Muslims believe that the entire Quran was revealed in Prophet Muhammad's (S:) lifetime, albeit at different times and places, and that he compiled the suras according to their verses and relevant meanings. It is also accepted that the Prophet obeyed only God's instructions, and did not act on his own accord regarding the compilation of the Quran. Therefore, it can be suggested that divine order guided the Prophet in arranging the suras and their verses. The author hypothesizes that the pyramid structure found in the text of the Quran is an intentional design created by God, the Supreme Artist.

(ii) *Graphic Design as Composed through the Stages of Human Existence*

The various stages of human life described in the Quran can be represented as a graph, as the author discovered when searching for artistic styles intrinsically present within the text. The patterns are represented as lines and dots (see Figure 8), and depict man's physical and mental development, as described in several parts of the Quran. The diagram shows that human life starts with the command of God and after journeying through various stages joins an eternal afterlife following its inevitable death. The message is simple: there is a beginning to everything, except God, and there is an end to everything, except God. The author, through a combination of Quranic and current secular knowledge, sketched this schematic design of human life . The suras in each of the stages 1 to 11 shown in Figure 8 are discussed in detail next.

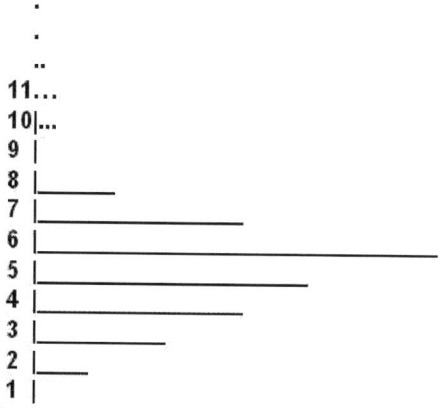

Identity Through Science, Philosophy and Artistic Concepts in the Quran

```
  .
  .
  ..
11...
10|...
 9 |
 8 |_____
 7 |_____
 6 |_____
 5 |_____
 4 |_____
 3 |_____
 2 |____
 1 |
```

1. Beginning = without mortal existence
2. Second stage = beginning of mortal existence
3. Growth of knowledge = growth of mind
4. Growth of knowledge = growth of mind = human maturity through stages
5. Growth of knowledge = growth of a mature mind
6. Power = ultimate growth through achievements
7. Old age
8. Inactivity / feebleness
9. Death = end of mortal existence
10. Eternal life = beyond mortal existence
11. The dots in the graph from this point onwards represent the fading of mortal life, which is no longer in one form but in fragments dissipating into its eternal phase.

Figure 8. Graphical representation of human life.

<u>Stage 1</u>   'The beginning of life at God's Order'   (84.19)

<u>Stage 2</u>   'Blank stage, when the baby is in the mother's womb with no identity'   (45.13; 76.1; 82.7–8)

<u>Stage 3</u>   'Growth of Knowledge': Concept of Environments
    (a) Domestic environment, e.g. 'fruits, trees, grains'   (71.14)
    (b) Space/external environment, e.g. 'sun, moon, sky'   (30.54; 71.14)

<u>Stage 4</u>   'Growth of Knowledge': Concept of individual identity

	'Body, Mind and Soul together create human identity'	(30.54)
Stage 5 materials	'Growth of Knowledge': Human growth from earthly 'wealth, fame', etc.	(71.14)
Stage 6	'Possession of Power/Height of Manhood'	(30.54)
Stage 7	'Old age'	(30.54; 36.68)
Stage 8	'Old and not active (feeble)'	(16.70; 30.54)
Stage 9	'Death'/end of mortal life	(21.35)
Stage 10	'Continuity of life in eternity'	(28.70)
Stage 11	'God disposes all things in perfect order'	(27.88)

Just as in the pyramid design, the above schematic model of human life projects a sublime sense of art in the Quranic composition.

2) Beautiful Expressions: Beauty, Precision and Reality in the Quran

In this section only a few Quranic examples have been selected for discussion. What is striking about these examples is the simplicity and clarity of language, which is sometimes charming, sometimes strong and at other times direct, practical and even mystical. This is a language that is ideal for perusal by the average person as well as for the intellectual analysis of the elite. It is a universal language for all of mankind.

These Quranic verses are divided into two groups:

Group One - Creative Quranic Art with Realism: The Prophet Muhammad (S:)

Group Two - Mystical Art and its Relevance to Prophet Muhammad (S:)

Group One

Beauty and Realism in the Creative Quranic Art: Allah's Messenger Prophet Muhammad(S:)

Descriptions of the Prophet Muhammad's (S:) life can be found all over the Quran. These narratives are vividly descriptive, and it is possible to paint a clear artistic impression of his life, endeavours and personality through a compilation of these verses.

The Quran was revealed as a series of lectures or 'Furqan', as it is known in the Quran, for a *single* pupil, who performed all his divine duties on his own. The pupil was trained in such a way that he could take over the burden of teaching, law-making, administrating a new nascent community and securing the state almost single-handedly. The author believes that the greatest art in the Quran is some of the captivating expressions revealed by Allah to Prophet Muhammad (S:). By looking at examples of some of these expressions we can gain insight into the extraordinary and divine teaching methods that bonded the Supreme Artist and His observant pupil.

We discussed at the beginning of this chapter how Allah as the Artist is the 'Reality' and Prophet Muhammad (S:) is the central figure in His 'Art', the Quran. Although there is no historical or scientific method that has proved that the person described in the Quran is indeed Prophet Muhammad (S:), and his existence is only in the faithful believer's mind, are there ways in which we can establish his identity in the twenty-first century?

It has been said that the truth of an age can be assessed through the art of that age, be it as fine art, craft or a traditional way of storytelling [309] [310]. Since the Quran is historically accepted as being contemporary to the period when Prophet Muhammad (S:) lived [311], we can assert that the existence of that period in itself verifies the Prophet's time through the Quranic text. Similarly, *time* is sometimes expressed in the Quran in the present tense to qualify certain verses describing the person 'Muhammad'. For the author this creates a feeling of visual reality, just as an artist's bright stroke of colour on the canvas would.

In the seventh century the Arabian Peninsula did not have a tradition of preserving art and culture through painting – a practice which would obviously provide visual evidence of the past. Nevertheless, Arabia had developed a rich style of poetry that offers us an informative assessment of the culture of that age. Their verbal or oral-based tradition of citing the 'good name' of the family fitted well into the artistic style of pre-Quranic Arabia. Subsequently, the Quran followed the same tradition of storytelling using a chronological style to sketch a portrait of Prophet Muhammad (S:) as an individual [312]. Although the artistic style is not precisely historical we can collect references about the Prophet from the Quran and use it to outline him within the historical context of that period and land. In other words, the Quran as a piece of *art* with a *man*, namely Prophet Muhammad (S:), at the centre is also a social representation of that age [313] [314].

The author believes that certain narrations of the Prophet's personal life reflect a masterstroke in the Quranic style. These verses take the reader into the Prophet's intimate surroundings using the present tense while indicating the contemporary period of seventh-century Arabia (see ref. 129). The style and verses create location and settings from where a glimpse of the Prophet's outfit, his habits, the name of one of his family members, his social standing in the community and the ability to settle disputes all become real to us. These interesting details from the verses provide us with a powerful and practical description of the person who became Allah's Rasul and last messenger.

The description of events found in the Quran has been arranged in a symbolic manner, starting with the Prophet's early life and continuing until his spiritual self reaches full maturity. The Quranic verses below

Identity Through Science, Philosophy and Artistic Concepts in the Quran

outline Prophet Muhammad's (S:) life using remarkable artistic style:

1. 'for the protection of Qureish: their protection in their summer and winter journeying' (106.1)

The Prophet belonged to the Qureishi family, which was mainly confined to Makkah. In seventh-century Arabia the Qureishi tribe in Hijaj were influential businessmen and had authority over many matters. The Quranic reference to this tribe and their biannual caravan trips abroad for business provides an impression of the Prophet's family background and his early life.

2. 'did He not find thee an orphan and protect (thee)?
   Did He not find thee wandering and direct [thee]?
   Did He not find thee destitute and enrich [thee]?'
   (93.6–8)
   'this is clear Arabic speech' (20.112–114; 42.7; 43.1)

According to tradition, the Prophet Muhammad (S:) became an orphan at the age of six. He was brought up by a number of relatives and by his mid-twenties was an independent man conversed in the art of business. As pointed out in the Quran, he was helped by Allah to achieve a life of plenty.

As we know, Prophet Muhammad (S:) originated from Arabia, and therefore his mother tongue was Arabic.

3. 'God made the Kabah the sacred house, an asylum of security for men' (3.96)
   'And thou art an in-dweller [resident] of this city' (90.1)
   'We made the House [at Makkah] for resort and a sanctuary for mankind, saying: "Make the place where Abraham stood a house of worship"'
   (5.100; 29.67)

Prophet Muhammad (S:) was a freeman from Makkah, the city where the Kabah was built. It is believed that it is in this city of (pre-Quranic) idol worshippers that the Prophet first started his preachings and where the beginning and early development of Islam took place. The Kabah also connects Prophet Muhammad (S:) to other messengers who followed in the footsteps of Abraham (S:).

4. **'Even as thy Lord caused thee** [Muhammad] **to go forth from thy home with the truth'** (8.5)
   'and among those around you (O Muhammad) are hypocrites, and so are some of the citizens of Medina' (33.9–27)
   'will surely bring you home again' (28.85)

Following persecution in Makkah for his preachings, the Prophet (and his followers) migrated to today's Medina as a Muhajirun, or immigrant. Further developement of Islam took place at this time, and the Quran warns the Prophet about his activities amongst the Medinite people attracting phoney supporters.

It is interesting to note that the Quran gives assurance to Prophet Muhammad (S:) that he would return home to Makkah from his exile in Medina.

5. **'those who follow the Apostle who can neither read nor write'** (7.157)
   'thus do We make plain Our revelations, that they may say: "You have studied deep"' (6.105; 98.2)

The wisdom in the Quran not only covered problems present in everyday life, but also encompassed many other incidents and occurrences that can be understood only by in-depth study of the subject. The Prophet could neither read nor write the Arabic language and is referred to as 'unlettered' in the Quran. He was nevertheless tutored initially through simple Quranic messages explaining the spiritual and

Identity Through Science, Philosophy and Artistic Concepts in the Quran

universal knowledge of life, and subsequently he was tutored in more profound ideas of wisdom which he conveyed to his followers. This tutoring helped him to convey both ordinary and profound messages from God, and to clarify the relationship between the Creator and His creation.

6. 'We shall make you recite Our revelations, so that you shall forget none of them except as God pleases' (87.6; 98.2)

Once the Quranic revelations came to Prophet Muhammad (S:) he recited and memorized them, in keeping with the verbal or oral-based Arab tradition of that time. Such Quranic direction would have ensured an accurate recording of the knowledge received from God.

7. 'Lo We have revealed it, a lecture in Arabic, that ye may understand' (165.1)

The Quran makes it clear that the Prophet would have a comprehensive understanding of God's words and commands because the revelations were in Arabic. Subsequently, preaching in his mother tongue to Arabic speakers would have been useful for the Prophet.

8. 'There has now come to you an apostle of your own, one who grieves at your sinfulness and cares for you; one who is benevolent and merciful to true believers –, – and guides them like a shining light' (33.21, 46)

These verses from the Quran describe the role of Prophet Muhammad (S:) more clearly. He was expected to provide guidance to his followers and countrymen, as well as care for them.

9.   'And We sent not [as Our Messenger] before thee other than men whom we inspired – nor were they immortals – then We [Allah's majestic power in a plural sense] **fulfilled the promises unto them'**   (40.77; 42.3)

He was also given knowledge on other past prophets, who were mortals like him, and obeyed God's command.

10.   **'Fighting is obligatory for you, much as you dislike it'** – **'Make war on them until idolatry shall cease'**   (15.89–99)

It seems that Prophet Muhammad (S:) was commanded by the Quran to declare war on idolatry and the tribes involved in idol worshipping, although he did not like wars. In seventh-century Arabia war may have been the only way to stop idolatry and to establish Islam.

11.   **'God had already given you victory at Badr when you were helpless'**   (3.123)
    'God had aided you on many a battlefield. In the battle of Hunain you set great store by your numbers'   (9.25)

Historical fighting in places like Badr and Hunain is mentioned in the Quran during which war between the Prophet's men and his enemies took place.

12.   **'Remember how you fled in panic while the Apostle at your rear was calling out to you. Therefore He paid you back with sorrow for every vexation'**   (8.7–17; 33.13)

Interestingly, conflicts between the Prophet's supporters and non-Muslims, during which the Prophet was humiliated and the Muslims lost the battles, were also recorded in the Quran.

13. 'Verily We have granted you a glorious victory' (48.1)

The Quran describes the peace treaty of Hudaibyia between the Qureish of Makkah and the Medinite Muslims led by the Prophet as the *victory*. The taking of Makkah was in the sixth AH (after hijrat), which corresponds to about AD 628.

14. 'When God's help and victory come, and you see men embrace God's faith in multitudes, give glory to your Lord and seek His pardon' (110.1–3)

Finally, after the fall of Makkah, the Quran declared that Prophet Muhammad's (S:) mission was concluded. That is, Islam had been brought to Makkah and the idolators had been defeated.

15. 'Lo thou art of those sent on a straight path –'
(35.23; 36.1; 42.15, 52)

'– as a warner and bringer of glad tidings' (7.188; 48.8)

The Quran depicts Allah's Messenger as an upright person who is not only the bearer of good news but gives warnings against misdeeds. The Prophet's duty is to caution people against making mistakes, to advise man to witness God's ways and to help people discover and understand the Creator both in the context of his or her surroundings as well as his or her inner self. The Prophet was expected to carry out this duty by spreading the knowledge he had gained through Quranic inspiration to his followers. He had to deliver the Quranic wisdom to the world as good news and glad tidings.

16. 'Lo with hardship goeth ease, so when thou art relieved, still toil and strive to please thy Lord' (94.4)

'He frowned and turned away, because the blind man came unto him' (80.1)

'It is part of the mercy of God that thou dost deal gently with them' (3.159)

The Prophet's life in the Quran describes hardship, persecution, humiliation and finally migration from his homeland of Makkah. Despite his distress, the Quran is not lenient about the Prophet's actions, although certain suras sometimes provide a comforting solace from God. It is interesting to note how the Quranic verses do not shy away from being critical when Prophet Muhammad (S:) misjudges a situation, as in the above example of a meeting with a blind man.

17. **'In the Apostle of God there is a beautiful pattern of conduct'** (33.21)

    'Believers, do not raise your voices above the voice of the Prophet, nor shout aloud when speaking to him as you do to one another' (49.2–3)

The Quran also paints another picture of the Prophet Muhammad (S:). We find him to be a gentle, kind and enduring person who guides his followers to God, and who should be respected by community members.

18. **'Cloaked one'** (74.1)

According to the Quran the Prophet wrapped a cloak around him as part of his customary dressing.

'Enshrouded one' (73.1)

Whenever Prophet Muhammad (S:) had revelations he used to feel cold and covered himself; this action seems to have been recorded in the Quran.

'Abu Lahab'
(111.1)

Historical records show that an uncle of the Prophet was called Abu Lahab. He is documented as being anti-Allah and, notably, pursued anti-Islamic strategies.

'She that disputeth'
(58.1)

As an example of the range of issues that he had to deal with, the Quran quotes an event in Medina when a woman asked the Prophet to settle a domestic matter.

Another point of discussion on Prophet Muhammad (S:) is how the identity of a person from that era was created not only through precise descriptions, but also by qualifying his character with details of his background and the actions he took in his life. This is an astute way of sketching his life with all the extra touches, which makes the picture more realistic and appealing to the audience.

The above narration started from Prophet Muhammad's (S:) orphaned childhood, then ambled along different paths, finally leading us to his victory and the fulfilment of his goal. Moreover, the Quran's 'storytelling' style in the present tense paints a realistic view of his surroundings and personal habits or clothes. Therefore the style of these verses helps create the central character, the Prophet, so that his *person* not only stands out as *real* in the Quran, but his era, his status and his life are also portrayed as part of the history of seventh-century Arabia.

Just as in a great piece of art such descriptive verses create a lasting impression on the hearts and minds of the faithful; the skill of the artist, in this case Allah, is timeless and helps to bring the reality of the past to the twenty-first century.

SUCCESSFUL ARTIST

The human mind seeks tranquillity and eternal peace by attempting to understand the mysterious Creator, and to some extent prayer serves this purpose. But the yearning to feel complete finally comes through submission to God [315] [316], because it creates a sense of fulfilment from within.

In the conclusion of his essay 'The World as I See It', Albert Einstein presented an idea in which the mysterious became the source of science, art and religion. In his words: 'it is the fundamental emotion which stands at the cradle of true art and true science – a knowledge of the existence of something we cannot penetrate – it is this knowledge and emotion that constitute the truly religious attitude' ('The Mysterious', excerpts from 'The World as I See It' by Einstein).

The author believes that the above quotation corresponds well with the Prophet's Quranic prayers quoted below. Since Quranic verses are mostly for the expression of human emotions, these prayers teach the shattered, confused and desperate mind how to ask for God's help and guidance. At other times the prayers are in praise of God. These verses are poetic and describe the Prophet's love for the Creator in a language radiating grace and charm that would interest inquisitive minds. Many of Prophet Muhammad's (S:) prayers from the Quran are in awe and wonder of the Creator – akin to hymns. These prayers, of which only a few are quoted here, come as a submission to the absolute and unknown mystery of Allah.

Some of these Quranic prayers give us a chance to observe in the words of the Quran how this exceptional *art*, the Prophet Muhammad (S:) himself, is yearning to unite with his *Creator the Artist*.

'I bow to God [in Islam]' (6.162)
'Lo! my worship and my sacrifice –
and my living and my dying are for Allah, –
Lord of the universe' (6.162)
'He is the first and the last, –
and the outward and the inward;

And he is the Knower of all things' (57.3)
'Lo! I am of those who surrender [unto Him]' (41.33)

Thus, almost in a circular manner, this created *art* tries to contact his own sublime source, the Creator, His achievements and accomplishments. Prophet Muhammad (S:) seems not only certain of this *Absolute* presence but is mystified and humbled by it too. According to the Quran such a sense of submission identifies an individual who has finally completed the search for his identity. The individual's life is therefore fulfilled and complete from within, which is satisfactory to God, the Artist.

'Truly did God fulfil the vision for His Apostle' (48.27)
'Muhammad is the Apostle of God' (48.29)

These two verses from sura 48 are called 'Victory'. They allow us to appreciate how the Prophet's followers may have felt when the ultimate objective of the Quran was revealed through essentially an ordinary person who, like them, led a mundane life and undertook daily chores. These revelations convey the Artist's opinion of His creation by declaring that the mission was complete; also, Prophet Muhammad's (S:) surrender and submission to God are accepted. The Prophet's humility, in the eyes of God, combined with his complete faith in the Creator, gained him the title 'Apostle of God'. Through this linguistic style the Quran expresses a sublime beauty and portrays a cordial relationship between Prophet Muhammad (S:) and God.

A PLACE IN HISTORY

Although this chapter looks at the artistic style in the Quran it is worth emphasizing that historically Prophet Muhammad (S:) influenced Arabian society immensely in its political, administrative and legislative orders. As a result people from near and far became interested in knowing how seventh-century Arabia had undergone this change within such a short period.

In the last period of the Prophet's life, and after his death around AD 632, oral traditions and travellers' tales started associating the name *Muhammad* with the pioneering role in the new social order created in Arabia. In this way the Prophet and the Quran became linked to the Arabian soil and its history. The earliest such record can be found in an Armenian chronicle from the AD 660, in quotes from Jewish refugees from Edessa who were saved from the Persians by Heraclius around AD 628. The Bishop Sebeos recorded in a chronicle the stories recounted by refugees about the Prophet's influence in Arabia.

According to this story there was an Ishmaelite called *Mahmet* in Arabia, who was a merchant but became a preacher and taught the Arab people about Abraham's God and monotheism. He was well informed and united his people [317]. Today it is easy to wonder at the strength of his personality, his eminent political gifts and his power to influence those around him. The conclusion drawn by modern critics is that Prophet Muhammad's (S:) conviction concerning one God and his compelling authority are the clues to his extraordinary success. The Quran remained the sole *miracle* of the 'unlettered' or 'illiterate' Arabian Prophet [318]. The Quran, through its unique expressions, not only proved to be a lecture but also established Muhammad (S:), the Quran's central character, as the Prophet from Arabia and thereby secured him a place in history.

<u>Group Two</u>

BEAUTIFUL AND MYSTICAL ARTISTIC QURANIC EXPRESSIONS - RELEVANCE FOR THE PROPHET MUHAMMAD (S:)

'Have we not caused thy bosom to dilate and eased thee
Of the burden
Which weighed down thy back' (94.1–4)
'By the fig and olive
By Mount Sinai
And by this land made safe' (95.1–3)
'Who will give a generous loan to God?

He will pay him back twofold
And he shall receive a noble recompense' (57.10–11)
'The Calamity
What is the Calamity?
Ah, what will convey unto thee what the Calamity is' (101.1–2)
'The Reality
What is the Reality?
Ah, what will convey unto thee what the Reality is?'
(69.1–3; 6.62)

The above group of verses are philosophical and often rhetorical, and will appeal to the incisive mind. What is their relevance to Prophet Muhammad (S:)? What is their relevance to his teachings? Echoes from these mysterious verses can be found in recent articles such as 'Maybe the Nature of Reality Is Hidden from Us' [319]. Perhaps further research and studies from within the scientific, philosophical and religious communities might one day help us to understand these verses in greater depth.

2.

Art in Nature – The Quranic Concept

LIFE AND NATURE IN CREATIVE ART - THE LIVING WORLD

These Quranic verses are divided into several groups:

- ❖ The Natural and Domestic Life of Man.
- ❖ Nature Related to Life.
- ❖ Beauty, Precision and Quranic terms.
- ❖ Beauty and Chaos Compared to Quranic Expressions.
- ❖ Man-made Art.

The Natural and Domestic Life of Man

Some verses from the sura or chapter 'Rahman', i.e. the All-Merciful or the Beneficent, give us a glimpse of the beauty, precision and realism in Quranic expressions. They declare that whichever way we turn, we can see God's creations within a precise and balanced design. At the same time this style creates a beautiful vision of a place full of fragrance from **'scented herbs'** (55.10–13) and gives a sense of domestic peace and tranquillity. The sura also points out that our mortal life will end through death. The verses are as follows:

'The All Merciful has taught the Quran. He created man and taught him the Explanation [via man's power of articulated speech, intelligence and self-expression]'
(55.1–4)
'The sun and moon move along like clockwork
The stars and the trees adore
He raised the heaven on high and set the balance of all things,
That you might not transgress that balance [by not exceeding the limit]' (55.5–8)
'He laid the earth for humanity, with all its fruits, and sheathed palm trees, husked grain and scented herbs
So which of your Lord's bounties would you deny?'
(55.10–13)
'All that lives on earth is doomed to die. But the face of your Lord will abide forever, in all its majesty and glory'
(55.26–27)

Generally, seventh-century writings made the public aware of the many wonders achieved by humans, and these ultimately led to 'hero-worshiping'. Storytelling, drawing and hero-worshipping were integral components of the culture, and the narrative style of sura 'Rahman' comes into the storytelling category. Therefore, the Quranic style of explaining simple information in different ways and its practical approach to philosophical teachings were welcomed because they were felt to be presenting enthusiastic new ideas in a unique way. This fresh new approach also helped to inspire the hearts and minds of people from all strata of life. This was possibly because people identified with the realistic views of many important aspects of domestic and public life portrayed in the Quran. The author believes that individuals from all ages would feel a natural affinity to and identify with such narrations.

Nature Related to Life

The following verses contain some of the artistic relationships in nature described in the Quran:

'In the water which God sends down from the sky
And with which He revives* the earth after its death,*
In the disposal* of the winds, and in the clouds that are
driven* between sky and earth'
(2.164)

(* Note that the words 'revives' and 'death' are contrasts, while the words 'disposal' and 'driven' qualify each other.)

'He created the beasts which give you warmth* and food
And other benefits,*
How pleasant* they look when you bring them home
And rest
And when you lead them out to pasture'
(16.6)

(* Note that the words 'warmth', 'benefits' and 'pleasant' supplement each other.)

'In the mountains there are streaks of various shades
Of white* and red,*
And jet black* rocks
Men and beasts and cattle have their colours too'
(35.27–28)

(* Note the beautiful arrangement of the words 'white', 'red' and 'jet black'.)

'The spring is a cool* bath and a refreshing* drink'
(38.43)

(* Note the complementary link between the words 'cool' and 'refreshing'.)

'Has made the night as a robe* for you and sleep as a repose* and makes the day as resurrection*'
(25.47)

(* Note the meaning of 'robe' and 'repose' convey the idea of comfort and tranquillity or rest, whereas the word resurrection is connected to renewal and revitalization.)

The above verses are examples of the superb clarity, simplicity and vividness that exist within the Quranic text. Such expressions are composed in a poetic style based on the realistic phenomena of human life and the natural world. Both the subject and the style allow us to easily understand and accept these ideas.

The author has given below a number of examples of natural phenomena from the Quran:

'By the heaven holding mansions of the stars
By the heaven and the morning star

Ah what will tell thee what the morning star is!
The piercing star!'
(86.1–2)

'We made the night and the day twin marvels'
(17.11)

'We enshrouded the night with darkness
and gave light to the day'
(89.1)

'Veil of night over the day'
(7.54)

'And the night when it withdraweth
And the dawn when it shineth forth'
(74.33–34)

'The dawn breathes away the darkness'
(81.180)

'By the light of the day and by the dark of night'
(93.1)

'By the sun and his midday brightness,
 By the moon which rises after him, by the day which reveals his splendour;
 By the night which veils him'
(91.1–5)

Shams Un Nahar Zaman

'The sun is a lamp and the moon is a light'
(71.16)

'By the emissary winds one after another
 By the raging hurricanes'
(78.1–2)

'By the dust scattering winds and the heavily laden clouds'
(51.1)

'God drives the clouds, then gathers and piles them up in masses
Which pour down torrents of rain'
(25.48)

'From heaven mountains He sends down hails'
(24.43)

'Drives the winds heralding the approach of His mercy'
(25.48)

'He has let loose the two oceans; they meet one another.
Yet between them stands a barrier
Which they cannot overrun'
(55.19–20)

'Sent the two seas rolling,
The one sweet and fresh,
The other salt and bitter and set a rampant between them,
An insurmountable barrier'
(25.53)

The author feels that the above Quranic verses express superbly various phenomena from the natural world. The juxtaposition of words in the style of the Quran has created visions not only of serene beauty but of beauty in real life. Contemporary minds may question whether these words are artistic. The author would argue that these verses are a form of art because they create a lasting impression of the beauty of nature and the universe. We can therefore claim that the Quranic language has an artistic status. The vividness of the language through which the art is taking shape makes it possible to grasp the nearness of God. The language is simple and yet descriptive, as though it is to be used to teach a small child. We can compare the similarities between scientific techniques and artistic drawings and focus on how modern scientific ideas aim to impress themselves on a child's vision of the world [320] [321]. The search for human identity gets a boost from the above verses as they not only represent nature but the nurturer of our universe.

Beauty, Precision and Quranic Terms

'Everything is in a measured quantity'
(54.49; 67.3)
'This creation is in exact precision'
(13.8; 15.21; 67.3)
'Creation is in due proportion'
(10.20; 27.88; 82.7; 80.19)

Mathematics has a close link with arts [322] [323]. For instance, the study of patterns is best described through mathematics following the Quran's assertion that **'everything is in a measured quantity'** (54.49; 67.3). There is something fundamental in the mathematical event which creates patterns stretching between nothing and infinity. Whereas art and science have ways in which to validate themselves, there is a role for art in science and vice versa. For example, art can play a part in science by helping in the visualization of an idea that cannot easily be explained [324] [325] [326].

Hundreds of years ago Islamic artists and architects found the secret of natural designs. They displayed this in their art through various geometrical patterns and architectures [327] [328]. Now, the discovery of *cosmic fractal* or geometrical patterns known as fractal designs has led modern cosmologists to assume that the cosmos or universe follows precise laws in all natural phenomena, e.g. in the creation of clouds and snowflakes, in cosmic patterns. In other words there is, as suggested in the Quran, **'exact precision – due proportion'** in everything (13.8; 15.21; 67.3) (10.20; 27.88; 82.7; 80.19). Similarly, *scale-free networks* show that a few highly connected nodes or hubs are present in the networks over which the whole universal structure is spread [329]. The modern explanation of the fractal structure of the universe is possibly the key to *geometrical chaos patterns* that are found to exist in nature.

The main feature in these designs, whether in nature or in Islamic architecture, is the breakdown of a single pattern into several different sizes and shapes, or unity and diversity. Some of the broken-down fractals form designs which repeat the old pattern, while others form new patterns. In this way, with every break from the main node or hub, another similar node or hub, as well as some different designs, is produced. The Quranic idea **'some are the same and some are different'** (6.99, 100) is applicable here.

In the same way we can find vivacious displays of colours in nature, such as in the rainbow, in the wings of a butterfly or in a sunflower. Although these patterns are artistically beautiful, they have led scientists and mathematicians to search for the underlying chemistry and formulae for these designs. Enrico Coen, trying to explain the elegant curves and designs in leaves, established that geometry played an important part in nature (see ref. 326). What is notable is that scientific knowledge is gradually able to unfold the secrets behind nature's beauty.

We can therefore say that humans are now able to connect beauty with the truth of mathematics and science [330], and as both subjects observe and deal with the laws of nature, we can agree with the verse **'this creation is in exact precision – in due proportion'** (13.8; 15.21; 67.3) (10.20; 27.88; 82.7; 80.19). Man's knowledge and activities (e.g. in mathematics, geometry, science) give him a position in God's world; here man can identify himself as another creation which has precision and proportion.

CHAOS, A NATURAL PHENOMENON WITH COMPARABLE QURANIC EXPRESSIONS

'Allah created other unknown things' (31.20)
'raging hurricanes' (78.1–2)

The modern age has produced many artists who have created art after being inspired by the ferocious forces of nature. Some of these works are referred to as the 'art of chaos' [331] [332]. The artistic beauty in such work comes from the balance between order and disorder, e.g. the shape of a turbulent tornado. A hurricane or a tornado, through its sheer natural, force creates a beauty that whirls around, breaking all boundaries but remaining ferocious and careless in nature. The untamed power within hurricanes and their degree of chaos can be calculated mathematically, but the *feeling* of their ferocity has yet to be calculated. These Quranic words, **'unknown'** (31.20) and **'raging hurricanes'** (78.1–2), paint a realistic picture of the unfathomed and violent nature of the hurricane, which is deep and unsympathetic on the one hand, but beautiful in another way.

'the depths of darkness in a vast deep ocean, overwhelmed with layer topped by layer of waves, topped with dark clouds' (24.40)

An *expressionist* painting exhibited at the Tate Modern Collection in 2006, called *The Sea B* by Emil Nolde (1867–1956), reminded the author of the feeling expressed in the above Quranic verses about the ocean. Both compositions characterized a deep turbulent ocean topped with dark clouds. The verses and the painting are both suggestive of a great wild storm broiling on the horizon which is awe inspiring and beyond human control. One was formed from the close contiguity of simple words in the Arabian desert in the seventh century, whilst the other was created with paint and brush by a nineteenth-century European artist.

This expressive Quranic description is in itself a form of art. The image's **'depths of darkness – topped with dark clouds'** (24.40) paints an everlasting picture of beauty and power in the human mind. Emil Nolde's account of the painting also gives a brilliant picture: 'I wanted to see the sea – in all its wild greatness – thunderous clouds came, driven by hail-storms – lightning flashed into the sea – working on them in a state close to ectasy –'. This exposition of human ecstasy from the depth of Nolde's heart echoing nature's wildness corresponds well with the above Quranic verse.

3.
Art Representing Mankind – the Quran's Influence

HUMAN KNOWLEDGE IN ART

A true piece of art is a timeless piece of work that maintains its originality and uniqueness. We know that the records of man's artistic nature go back many thousands of years, and the influences of history on the arts have been discussed already. Since tradition serves as the common ground between arts and craft we can say that art is part of the daily fabric of human life and society. It is widely recognized that visual arts from the dawn of history to the present day have had a large influence on human culture [333].

In the ancient world *magic* and *ritual* prompted the human mind to create images of animals which were often painted and sculpted on rock surfaces and in caves. Drawings and carvings were also made on bones. As mentioned earlier, people who lived in the Stone Age and ancient civilizations like the Bushmen of South Africa and the Aborigines of Australia have shown interest in the movement and physical nature of animals in their art. These artistic efforts probably represented the bond between man and animals that were close inhabitants of, and shared, the same habitat [334].

In the next stage of the human cultural evolution we find *architectural* development through art, such as the use of wood, brick and stone found in the New Stone Age cultures in tropical Africa

Identity Through Science, Philosophy and Artistic Concepts in the Quran

and the Americas [335]. During this age ancestral spirit worship was common and was represented through various forms of art. Paintings and sculptures also played an important role in the American medicine man's work in healing.

We know that at a later stage in human history writing developed as part of our artistic creations. When the Egyptian rulers or Pharaohs became the 'divine king', their life and, most crucially, their death were defined through artistic works. Paintings and writings glorified the pyramids, tombstones and works of architecture built by the Pharaohs. Furthermore, the ancient Near East and Mediterranean coastal areas like Iraq, Iran, Syria, Palestine, Turkey, Greece and Rome, as well as India, also developed distinct artistic cultures and customs between 3500 and 300 BC [336].

QURANIC IDEAS AND ISLAM'S INFLUENCE IN THE ARTS

The Islamic concept of art arises from the Quran, which guides us towards appreciating beauty and is central in stimulating creativity.

'God speaks through inspiration' (17.5; 6.122)
'Read thy Lord is the most Bounteous, Who teaches by the pen, teaches man which he knew not' (96.1–5)
'All things good, beautiful and useful are from God'
(10.2; 59.22–24)

These Quranic teachings act as a cultural philosophy and cornerstone for Muslims. The above verses, **'inspiration – read teaches'**, from the Quran encourage Muslims to believe that all knowledge is found or acquired successfully through God's help. This insight has allowed Muslim artists in the past and present to cultivate their interests in Islam and in art through the pursuit of knowledge.

The Islamic world has produced a variety of artistic works. However, the author believes that an artist with a Muslim name or a piece of art from a Muslim country alone cannot be categorized as *Islamic art*. Either the principle of Islam or the development of Islam needs to be the purpose of creating that art for the work to be considered as Islamic art. Similar opinions on this matter are also expressed by other Muslim writers [337].

Around the seventh century the Asian land route known as the Old Silk Route crossed the Mediterranean to Iran, Turkestan, the Tarim basin, India, South-East Asia and finally into China. Islam spread along this route and brought together different artistic sources and access to important cultural sites from around the Muslim world. The spiritual world was reflected through geometry and rhythm as well as through arabesque and calligraphy. Islam also introduced the practice of an iconic art that reflected the radiance of God.

Islam is considered to be the last monotheistic religion, and at its early developmental stage had inherited certain cultural characteristics from its predecessors, namely Judaism and Christianity, which also evolved within the same region [338]. Islamic paintings and sculptures are opposed to images of religious personages but non-religious representational art is accepted. As a result, landscapes became one of the favourite representations in such artwork while human or animal figures were forbidden, unless used for decorative purposes. Decorations with animal figures and decorative motifs of plants or geometrical figures were also used for artistic designs [339]. Geometrical designs in mosques, calligraphy and arabesque designs in the Quran and in other contexts have all been accepted as *Islamic art*.

In art, Islam inherited ideas from its predecessors in the regions where it flourished. Since Arabia at that time was not influenced by monumental architecture [340], at the beginning of its establishment neither Islam nor Muslims made any demands for visual artistic displays of their religion. However, gradually over time mosques and palaces became showpieces of artistic skills. In the Middle Ages, when Islam was spreading both in the East and the West, art represented the influence of Islamic culture. The power of a Muslim ruler and his kingdom was often displayed in their palaces, minarets or within mosques. Elaborate calligraphy and geometric patterns representing the divine Power and text within the Quran became channels for such artistic ventures. Granada in Spain, the Kutub Minar in Delhi or terracotta inscribed bricks in certain Bengal mosques are a few examples of this period. The decorations in mosques and their courtyards became part of the visual or spatial art in Islamic civilizations. The author has listed below the basic features of a mosque. The structure contains:

(a) a rectangular building with its main axis pointing towards Makkah;

(b) an enclosed courtyard surrounded by aisles that run towards the Kabah in Makkah;

(c) a small niche in the centre of the courtyard, the Mihrab; and

(d) the minaret to call the faithful to prayer. [341]

Kabah is considered to be the most important mosque for Muslims and is believed to be the place where God guided Prophet Abraham (S:) to pray in the **'Bakkah Valley'** (2.125). The centre of the Kabah mosque is taken worldwide as the symbolic direction for prayer, or *Qibla*, for prayers performed at mosques or within the home. The second-most important mosque for Muslims is the one whose original structure was built at Medina by Prophet Muhammad (S:) and his associates.

Throughout history, the calligraphy of Quranic art remained mainly as a decorative style of writing the Arabic script. Gradually, flexible sets of shapes and geometric curvilinear designs became popular in the Muslim world and developed into the discipline of abstract art we know today [342]. It has long been thought that for Muslims to be nearer to God they need to learn Arabic and recite the Quran in Arabic. Following this idea hand-calligraphed Qurans constituted one of the greatest artistic heritages of the Islamic world. Like the Quran, the prayer rug or mat also became an artistic conduit in the hands and the minds of Muslim craftsmen with many designs, shapes and styles of calligraphy decorating the rug, which they still do today [343].

Similarly, in the light of **'all things good, beautiful and useful are from God'** (10.2; 59.22–24), music, which is an artistic expression of the human soul, is taken in many parts of the world, including the Muslim world, as a power to move the faithful towards God [344].

The author believes that music can uplift the spirit (of the faithful) to the realms of eternity. So that the Quran's poetic verses, God's praise or silent meditation of the Absolute Creator are all meant to touch the human soul and break the boundaries of the unfathomable, infinite Supreme Being. Islam's philosophy is that art and music knit the soul together on its journey. Through art, human identity becomes not just humble but also beautiful and purposeful.

Conclusion

This chapter on creative art has thrown some light on the development of the human aesthetic sense and how Quranic philosophies may have helped in this matter, especially in the Muslim world. The question of whether beauty can advance human perception of the inner self, where contentment eclipses all other emotion, has also been explored.

This chapter also relates Quranic art to some of its structural composition. The intrinsically beautiful and poetic Quranic language in its own artistic way portrays clearly, simply and vividly the beauty in nature and man. The author would suggest that although time and space hold all forms of ideas, they belong to the Creator, the greatest artist of all. Since time is a real entity, the genuinely creative artistic processes always function across time. Following this argument the author feels that the description of Prophet Muhammad's (S:) life is the best example of Quranic art. In this artistic expression, the Supreme Artist is not only creating a natural description of a living being, but is also presenting his life and his social surroundings as the final factor in the pursuit of human identity. The author would advocate that the journey to explore human identity is completed only when the soul submits totally to God from within. This act of submission has presented a realistic form of fulfilment and contentment for humans through the ages.

Conclusion

In order to understand the Quranic vision for mankind, which is relevant in the present world we need to interpret its scientific, philosophical and artistic ideas in a contemporary fashion. The human figure depicted in the Quran represents mankind across infinite cultures or time, and the search for human identity takes the style and pace of a narrative.

The Quran's simple language, clear ideas and multiple meanings within verses make it easy and acceptable for use in a variety of human circumstances. Scientific, philosophical and artistic concepts from the Quran, as discussed in this book, can explain and predict many ideas which are central to modern times. Thus the Quran, far from being outdated, is relevant today and can be considered to be a timeless Book.

The observations from the Quran can be categorized into:

1. Natural laws, each with a beginning and an end, which are established by God to govern mankind and the universe.
2. The precise repetition of each law over time.
3. The harmonious existence amongst all living communities in nature.
4. Various *facts* which recognize the philosophical differences between individuals and communities.

5. Acknowledging and understanding God as the Supreme Creative Artist who helps us to find our inner self.

In its own exceptional way the Quran throws light in many directions, including on science, philosophy and arts. It discusses the physical and emotional hardships of mankind and offers solace under the guise of 'The Lecture'. In the author's opinion, the advances made in science, philosophy or artistic knowledge, whether independently or together, do not amount to much unless they benefit the human race as a whole. We can therefore assert that society is for **'increas**[ing] **knowledge** [with piety]' (20.114) and **'activity'** (36.58–68) while remaining **'in the middle path'** (6.115), and for thanking the **'Maker/Fashioner'** (28.12–14; 59.24). Surely, this is the real identity of humans today and addresses succinctly the question 'Who am I?'.

References

The following translations of the Holy Quran have been used:

1. A. Abdullah Yusuf ALI, *Holy Quran – English Translation*, 4th edn, vols 1 and 2, Kitab Khana Ishaat-ul-Islam, Delhi, 1978.
2. Muhammad Marmaduke PICKTHALL, *The Meanings of the Glorious Koran – English Translation*; Kitab Bhaban, New Delhi, 1992.
3. Arthur J. ARBERRY, *The Koran – Interpreted – Translated with an Introduction*, Oxford University Press, 1998.
4. N. J. DAWOOD, *The Koran – Translated with Notes*, Penguin, 1999.
5. T. B. IRVING, *The Quran – Translation*, Goodword Books, New Delhi, 2000.
6. Muhammad Habibur RAHMAN, *Koran Sutra/The Koranic References* (Bengali), Bangla Academy, 1984.
7. Mohammad Abdul ALEK, *A Study of the Quran – The Universal Guidance for Mankind*, M. A. Malek, 2000.
8. Bahram SAMI, *An Introduction to the Glorious Quran – the Book of Human Guidance*, Muhammadi Trust of Great Britain and NI, 1997.

9. Abdel M. A. S. HALEEM, *The Quran – a New Translation*, Oxford University Press, 2004.
10. Abdul Haleem M. ELLYASEE, *The Holy Quran with Arabic Text*, English translation, Islamic Book Service, New Delhi, 2001.
11. Mufazzal Hussain CHOWDHURY, *Teachings of the Final Revelation – a Compendium of Translation of and Commentary on the Glorious Quran by A. Yusuf Ali*, Computer Composing, 2003.

List of Further Reading

1. Karen ARMSTRONG, *A History of God*, Vintage, 1999.
2. M. A. J. BEG, *Islamic and Western Concepts of Civilization*, University of Malaya Press, Kuala Lumpur, 1982.
3. Dr Maurice BUCAILLE, *The Bible, The Quran and Science he Holy Scriptures Examined in the Light of Modern Knowledge*, translated from the French by Alaistair D. Pannell and the author, North American Trust Publications, 1978.
4. Dr Maurice BUCAILLE, *What Is the Origin of Man? The Answers of Science and the Holy Scriptures*, translated from the French by Alaistair D. Pannell and the author, North American Trust Publications, 1978.
5. Fritjof CAPRA, *The Turning Point – Science, Society and the Rising Culture*, Flamingo, 1987.
6. Dr S. M. DARSH, *Questions and Answers about Islam*, Ta-Ha Publishers, 1987.
7. Cyril GLASSE, *The Concise Encyclopaedia of Islam*, Introduction by Professor Huston Smith, Stacey International, London, 1989.

8. G. R. HAWTING, *The First Dynasty of Islam – the Umayyad Caliphate AD 661–750*, Croom Helm, London and Sydney, 1986.
9. Fazlur RAHMAN, *Islam*, 2nd edn, University of Chicago Press, London, 1979.
10. Tariq RAMADAN, *Western Muslims and the Future of Islam*, Oxford University Press, 2004.
11. Barnaby ROGERSON, *The Prophet Muhammad – a Biography*, Little, Brown, 2003.
12. Jonathan SACKS, *The Dignity of Difference – How to Avoid the Clash of Civilization*, Continuum, London and New York, 2003.
13. Mark S. SMITH, *The Origins of Biblical Monotheisms – Israel's Polytheistic Background and the Ugaritic Texts*, Oxford University Press, 2001.
14. Laura Veccia VAGLIERI, *An Interpretation of Islam*, translated from Italian by Dr Aldo Casseli, McGregor and Warner, Inc., Washington, DC, 1957.

Bibliography

Introduction

1. *The Oxford Popular English Dictionary*, 1998; p. 391.
2. *Encarta World English Dictionary*, Bloomsbury/Microsoft/Encarta, 1999; p. 934.
3. Mitchio KAKU, *Time Runs Forward*, BBC 4, 28.02.06.
4. Amanda GEFTER, 'The Riddle of Time', *New Scientist*, 15.10.05; pp. 31–3.
5. Fay DOWKER, 'Real Time Flows or Grows', *New Scientist*, 4.10.03.
6. Mitchio KAKU, *Life is Transient*, BBC 4, 12.03.04.
7. Fritjof CAPRA, *The Tao of Physics – An Exploration of the Parallels between Modern Physics and Eastern Mysticism*; 'Modern Physics – A Path with a Heart?', 3rd edn, Flamingo, 1991; p. 21.
8. John R. HINNELS, *Dictionary of Religions*, 1984; pp. 253–4.
9. Jean-Marie CHAUVET, Eliette Brunet DESCHAMPS, Christian HILLAIRE, *Chauvet Cave – The Discovery of the World's Oldest Paintings*; 'The Originality of the Chauvet Cave', Thames and Hudson, 1996; pp. 126, 127.
10. Mustafa CERIC, Grand Mufti Mustafa Reis ul-Ulama,

'Freedom of Spirit and Strength of Mind', *'Q' News*, 2004; p. 20.

11. Good News Bible, American Bible Society, 1976; Genesis 24, 25; p. 27.
12. William DALRYMPLE, 'More a Family Falling Out than a Clash of Civilizations', *Guardian*, 24.12.02.
13. Larry MITCHELL, *Biblical Hebrew and Aramaic Frequency List with Definitions, Pronunciation Guide and Index*, Academic Books, 1984; pp. 3, 4.
14. Good News Bible, 1976; Matt. 27.45; p. 44.
15. *The Jewish Bible, the JPS Translation according to the Traditional Hebrew Text*, Jewish Publication Society, Philadelphia, 1985; Tanakh; The Holy Scriptures; Torah: Exod. 3.9; p. 88.
16. Francis ROBINSON, *Atlas of the Islamic World since 1500*, Facts on File, 1992; 'The Quran'; p. 180.

The Quran

17. Ahmed VONDENFFER, *Ulum Al-Quran: An Introduction to the Sciences of the Quran; Collection of Revelations during the Prophet's Lifetime*, The Islamic Foundation, 1989; pp. 40–43.

Chapter One
Beginning: Islam and Medical Science in light of the Quran

18. HINNELS, 1984; pp. 208, 209.
19. Christopher de CHARMS, 'Power of the Mind Can Lessen Chronic Pain', *New Scientist*, 'Outlook on Life', 17.12.05; p.

19.

20. John McCRONE, 'Mental Gymnastics', *New Scientist*, 27.10.01; pp. 30–34.

21. Geoff WATTS, 'The Power of Nothing', *New Scientist*, 26.05.01; pp. 34–7.

22. Gerald J. TORTORA and Nicholas P. ANAGNOSTAKOS, *Principles of Anatomy and Physiology*, Figure 1: 'Human Blastocyst Attachment', Harper and Row, New York, 1987; p. 745.

23. Ibid.; pp. 747–9.

24. Ibid.; pp. 751–2.

25. Ibid.; p. 745.

26. Ibid.; p. 748.

27. Leon SCHLOSSBERG and George D. ZUIDEMA, 'The Menstrual Cycle', *The Johns Hopkins Atlas of Human Functional Anatomy*, Johns Hopkins University Press, 1977; pp. 88, 89.

28. TORTORA and ANAGNOSTAKOS, 1987, 'Chemical Compounds and Life Processes'; p. 33.

29. Imam NAWAWI Sharaf al-Din-Yahya ibn Sharaf, trans. with commentary by Dr Muhammad Yusuf ABBASI, *Forty Gems – Al-Arbaeen Sayings of the Holy Prophet*, Idara Isha at-E-Dinyat (P) Ltd, 1996; pp. 43–6.

30. Robert E. ROTHENBERG, *The New American Medical Dictionary and Health Manual*, Signet/New American Library, 1975; p. 270 .

31. Arthur GILLAUME, 'References to the Hypocrites and the Jews in the sura entitled "The Cow"', *The Life of Muhammad: A Translation of Ishaq's Sirat Rasul Allah*, Oxford University Press, 1990; p. 255.

32. TORTORA and ANAGNOSTAKOS, 1987, 'The Autonomic Nervous System'; p. 361.

33. William D. McELROY and Carl P. SWANSON, 'Introduction – The Growth of Science', 'The Science of Biology', 'The Evolution of Inherited Patterns', *Modern Cell Biology*, 2nd edn, Prentice Hall, Inc., Englewood Cliffs, NJ, 1976; pp. 12, 18, 315.

34. TORTORA and ANAGNOSTAKOS, 1987, 'Stress and Homeostasis'; p. 19.

35. William BOYD, 'Postmortem Changes', *A Text Book of Pathology – Structure and Function in Disease*, 8th (Asian) edn, Lea and Febiger, Philadelphia, 1977; pp. 44–5.

36. James B. WYNGARDEN and Lloyd H. SMITH, 'The Life Cycle Perspective in Medicine', 'Structural and Functional Changes with Age – Special Problems of Management', *Cecil Text Book of Medicine*, W. B. Saunders Company, 1982; pp. 27, 39.

37. TORTORA and ANAGNOSTAKOS, 1987, 'The Autonomic Nervous System'; p. 361.

38. Ann B. McNAUGHT and Robin CALLANDER, 'Absorption in Small Intestine', 'Transport of Absorbed Foodstuffs', *Illustrated Physiology*, 4th edn, Churchill Livingstone, 1984; pp. 70, 71.

39. TORTORA and ANAGNOSTAKOS, 1987, 'The Lymphatic System and Immunity'; pp. 530, 531.

40. G. H. BEATON and J. M. BENGOA, 'The Major Deficiency Syndromes, Epidemiology and Approaches to Control; Protein as Source of Amino Acid – Comparison of Chemical Scores', *Nutrition in Preventive Medicine*, World Health Organization, Geneva, 1976; p. 464.

41. Zafrullah Muhammad KHAN, 'Of His Drink', *The Prophet at*

Home, The London Mosque, 1967; p. 38.
42. Ibid.; p. 38.
43. Ibid.; 'Of His Food'; pp. 30–35.
44. Ibid.; pp. 30–33.
45. Ibid.; p. 32.
46. BEATON and BENGOA, 1976; p. 464.
47. Ralph WRIGHT, G. H. MILWARD-SADLER, K. G. M. M. ALBERTI and Stephen KARRAN, 'Alcoholic Liver Diseases', *Liver and Biliary Disease*, 2nd edn, Bailliere Tindall, W.B. Saunders Company, 1985; p. 882.
48. ABBASI, 1996; p. 164.
49. 'Food and Drink Habits in Obese Children', BBC 1 and Channel 4 News, December 2006.
50. SCHLOSSBERG and ZUIDEMA, 1977; pp. 88–9.
51. ABBASI, 1996; pp. 17, 69–71.
52. KHAN, 1967; p. 35.
53. AL-BUKHARI, *Sahi – Summarized Arabic–English*, trans. Dr Muhammad Muhsin Khan, Maktaba Dar-us-Salam, 1994; pp. 931–3.
54. Ibid.; p. 265.
55. Ibid.; pp. 266–7.
56. Ibid.; p. 145.
57. GILLAUME, 1990, 'The Rest of the Affair of Khayber'; p. 518.
58. Ibid.; p. 255.
59. TORTORA and ANAGNOSTAKOS, 1987; p. 570.
60. AL-BUKHARI, 1994; pp. 936–7.
61. Ibid.; pp. 940–41.
62. Ibid.; p. 938.
63. Ibid.; p. 917.

64. Ibid.; p. 939.
65. Batool ISPAHANY, 'Pain in the head', 'An invocation for pain in the belly', 'On fever and the manner of its treatment, water from the well of Zamzam', 'Disapproval of taking medications except when required, on lump sugar', 'For pain, cold, weakness in the abdomen, headache, back pain, oil of jasmine', 'Difficulty in childbirth', *Islamic Medical Wisdom – The Tibb al-Aimma*, ed. Andrew J. Newman, Muhammadi Trust, 1991; pp. 7–16, 22, 23, 57–9, 72–4, 75–8, 80, 87–121.
66. Peter HADFIELD, 'Women's Lib Got It Wrong in the 1970s', *New Scientist*, 5.10.02; p. 20.
67. Shams N. ZAMAN, review of and commentary on Abul Fadl Mohsin Ebrahim, *Organ Transplantation, Euthanasia, Cloning and Animal Experimentation – An Islamic View*, Islamic Foundation, 2001; *Muslim World Book Review*, 22(2), Jan.–Mar. 2002; p. 62.
68. Peter STANFORD, 'Praying for a More Spiritual Change', *Sunday Times*, 21.01.96.
69. Ibid.
70. WATTS, 26.05.01; see ref. 21.
71. Shams N. ZAMAN, Personal observations, King's College Hospital, Denmark Hill, London, 1994.
72. Anil ANANTHASWAMY, 'The Inner Strength that Keeps Women Going', *New Scientist*, 15.9.01.
73. Bryant FURLOW, 'The Enemy Within', *New Scientist*, 19.08.00.
74. Mitchell KRUCOFF, 'Prayers Fail to Help Heart Surgery Patients', *New Scientist*, 23.07.05.
75. Alison MOTLUK, 'Particles of Faith', *New Scientist*, 28.01.06.

76. James MEIKLE, 'Yoga Benefits Body, Soul and Blood Vessels', *Guardian*, 8.11.04.
77. Alexander CHANCELLOR, 'Heaven Up Here?', *Weekend Guardian*, 15.05.04.
78. M. SCOTT PECK, interviewed by Edward Marriott, 'Can a Guru Heal Himself?', *New Scientist*, 05.07.03.
79. Rowan HOOPER, 'If Meditation Is Good, God Makes It Better', *New Scientist*, 03.09.05.
80. Lisa MELTON, 'Use It Don't Lose It', *New Scientist*, 17.12.05.

Chapter Two
Limitations: Creation, Life and Activity

81. Paul DAVIES, 'Time and Space', *New Scientist*, 06.12.03; p. 34.
82. Michael CROSS, 'The Truth Is Out There', *New Scientist*, 'Inside Science', 19.02.00; pp. 1–4.
83. Ibid.
84. Robert IRION, 'Say the Magic Words', *New Scientist*, 09.06.01; pp. 32–5.
85. Editorial, 'The Hand of God', *New Scientist*, 28.09.01; p. 3.
86. Ameer ALI, 'The Ideal of Islam', *Spirit of Islam – A History of the Evolution and Ideals of Islam with Life of the Prophet*, A. One Publisher, Lahore, 1994; p. 112.
87. Muhammad Marmaduke PICKTHALL, *Cultural Side of Islam; Islamic Culture- Causes of Rise and Decline*, Kitab Bhaban, New Delhi, 1990; pp. 5, 11, 23.
88. Muhammad Marmuduke PICKTHALL, *The Meanings of the*

Glorious Koran, English trans., Kitab Bhaban, New Delhi, 1992.

89. Abdullah Yusuf ALI, *The Holy Quran*, English trans., vols 1 and 2, 4th edn, Kitab Khana, Delhi.

90. Muhammad A. IQBAL, 'Knowledge and Religious Experience', 'Human Ego – His Freedom and Immorality', *Reconstruction of Religious Thought in Islam*, Javid Iqbal, 1988; pp. 8–9, 16, 97.

91. Tariq RAMADAN, 'Who Are We? The Middle Path', *To Be a European Muslim*, 1999; pp. 184, 189, 191.

92. CROSS, 19.02.00; see ref. 82.

93. Jon TURNEY, 'What Is This Thing Called Science', *New Scientist*, 16.03.02; pp. 46–7.

94. CROSS, 19.02.00; see ref. 82.

95. MELTON, 17.12.05; see ref. 80.

96. Hazel CURRY, 'Mind over Matter', *Weekend Guardian*, 09.08.03.

97. Helen PHILIPS, commentary on John Allman, *The Cell that Makes Us Human*, *New Scientist*, 19.06.04.

98. TURNEY, 16.03.02; see ref. 93.

99. Jan MORRIS, 'Islam's Lost Grandeur', review of Mark Mazower, *Salonica, City of Ghosts: Christians, Muslims and Jews 1430–1950*, *Weekend Guardian*, 18.09.04.

100. Islamic Achievements: Islamic Expo 2006, Alexandra Palace, London, 07.07.06.

101. Jeff HECHT, 'And God Said Let There Be Smog', *New Scientist*, 24.08.02; p. 14.

102. Anil ANANTHASWAMY, 'North of the Big Bang', *New Scientist*, 02.09.06; pp. 28–31.

103. Marcus CHOWN, Backwards to the Future', *New Scientist*,

05.02.00; pp. 26–30.
104. Martin REES, 'Ripples from the Age of Time', *Guardian*, 24.04.92.
105. Charles ARTHUR, 'Scientists Capture the Colours of Creation', *Independent*, 29.03.96.
106. Paul DAVIES, 'What Happened before the Big Bang?', *Independent*, 03.06.95.
107. REES, 24.04.92; see ref. 104.
108. 'Atmosphere – the Earth's Screen', *Reader's Digest Atlas of the World*, 1990; p. 41.
109. Ken CROSWELL, 'Stellar Colour and Spectral Type', *New Scientist*, 'Inside Science', 26.11.94.
110. Larry O'HANLON, 'Snap, Crackle and Pop', *New Scientist*, 09.02.02; p. 6.
111. 'Asteroids', in Heather COUPER (ed.), *The Dorling Kindersley Science Encyclopedia*, Dorling Kindersley, London, 1998; p. 294.
112. Ibid., 'DNA Molecules'; p. 338.
113. Ibid.; p. 218.
114. Ibid.; pp. 372–3.
115. Ibid.; pp. 372–3.
116. Ibid.; pp. 372–3.
117. Paul DAVIES, 'Time and Space', *New Scientist*, 'Letter', 06.12.03; p. 34.
118. See ref. 107.
119. See ref. 108.
120. See ref. 84.
121. See ref. 85.
122. 'Life's First Letters', *New Scientist*, 'In Brief', 26.05.01; p. 27.
123. Jeff WIMBERLEY, 'Life Came from Rivers', *New Scientist*,

29.06.02; p. 27.
124. See ref. 29.
125. Ismail R. FARUQI and Lois Lamya FARUQI, 'Language and History – the Hebrews (19th–1st century BCE)', *The Cultural Atlas of Islam*, Institute of Islamic Thought, Collier Macmillan, New York, 1986; p. 38.
126. The Quran, sura 5, verse 12.
127. GILLAUME, 1990, 'The Poetry'; pp. xxv–xxx.
128. Albert HOURANI, 'A New Power in an Old World – Muhammad and the Appearance of Islam', *A History of the Arab Peoples*, Faber and Faber, 1991; p. 15.
129. Margaret WERTHEIM, 'God of the Quantum Vacuum', *New Scientist*, 04.10.97.
130. Keith WARD, 'Faith Based Science', *New Scientist*, 'Comment and Analysis', 27.11.04; p. 19.
131. Herman MELVILLE, 'The Last Word on Faith', *Guardian*, 24.06.04.
132. Michael BOND, interviewing Hussein al-Sharistani, *New Scientist*, 26.06.04; pp. 44–6.
133. Robert WINSTON, 'What Turns Us into Heroes', *Guardian*, 24.10.02.
134. Dan JONES, 'The Moral maze" *New Scientist*, 26.11.05; pp. 34–7.
135. REES, 24.04.92; see ref. 104.
136. Abd Al-Rahman AZZAM, 'The Islamic State – Some Basic Principles of the Islamic State', *The Eternal Message of Muhammad*, trans. Caeser E. Farah, Mentor, 1965; p. 105.
137. Annemarie SCHIMMEL, 'The Age of Iqbal', *Islam in the Indian Subcontinent*, E. J. Brill, Leiden/Cologne, 1980; p. 220.

Chapter Three
Relationships: Plants, Animals and the Human Species

138. Ahija Ali IZETVEGOVIC, 'Religion and Revolution', *Islam between East and West*, American Trust Publications, 1989; p. 60.
139. MUDROOROO, 'Introduction, All Mothers', 'Animal Behaviour', 'Katatjuta', *Aboriginal Mythology*, Aquarium/HarperCollins, 1994; pp. xi, 4, 90.
140. Mafi WILLIAMS, 'Spiritual Song of the Aborigine', *Spirit Songs; compiled by Lorraine; A Collection of Aboriginal Poetry*, Omnibus, 1993; p. 2.
141. Frank WATERS, 'Introduction', 'Spider Woman and the Twins', 'The Nature of Man', *Book of the Hopi*, 1997; pp. x, 4–5, 7.
142. Marlo MORGAN, 'Totems', *Mutant Message Down Under*, Thorsons/HarperCollins, 1994; p. 99.
143. Helen PHILIPS, 'Not Just a Pretty Face', *New Scientist*, 27.02.02; pp. 40–42.
144. Peter SUTTON, 'Big Genome', *New Scientist*, 'Letters', 03.08.02; p. 27.
145. Chris FRASER, 'Humans Are Animals', *New Scientist*, 29.06.02; p. 27.
146. Bob HOLMES, interviewed by Alexandra Morton, 'Call of the Wild', *New Scientist*, 21.11.02; pp. 46–9.
147. Adrian BARNETT, revieweing Eric Scigliano, *Nelly and Her Cousins*, *New Scientist*, 29.06.02; p. 56.
148. William McGREW, 'Hand Shaking Chimps Get to Grips with Culture', *New Scientist*, 14.04.01; p. 19.
149. Maggie McDONALD, interviewed by Cindy Engel, 'Animals

Can Teach Self Medication', *New Scientist*, 'Opinion Interview', 23.02.02; pp. 42–4.

150. James RANDERSON, 'Early Learning', *New Scientist*, 16.03.02; p. 11.

151. Culum BROWN, Robin DUNBAR, Alex KACELINK, Keith KENDRICK and Kate DOUGLAS, 'Animal Minds', *New Scientist*, 12.06.04; pp. 41, 42–3, 44–5, 46–7, 48–9, 52–3.

152. David ATTENBOROUGH, 'Bottle Nose Dolphin', *Blue Planet*, BBC TV, 2006, 2007.

153. Ken McNAMARA, 'Embryos and Evolution', *New Scientist*, 'Inside Science', 06.10.99; p. 3.

154. Robin ORWANT, 'What Makes Us Human', *New Scientist*, 21.02.04; pp. 36–9.

155. Antonio DAMASIO, 'Virtue in Mind', *New Scientist*, 08.11.03; pp. 49–51.

156. Antonio DAMASIO, 'Enfants Terribles', *The Economist*, 23.10.99; p. 156.

157. Ibid., 'Figure of Brain – Area for Learning Moral Language'; p. 156.

158. Owen FLANAGAN, 'The Colour of Happiness', *New Scientist*, 24.05.03; p. 44.

159. FARUQI and FARUQI, 1986, 'Arabia : The Crucible'; p. 18.

160. Hazel MUIR, 'Fly by the Stars', *New Scientist*, 09.02.02; p. 16.

161. Stanislas DEHAENE, 'Natural Born Readers', Figure 2, 'Human Brain "Word" Forming Area', *New Scientist*, 05.7.03; p. 32.

162. Andy COGHLAN, 'Not Such Close Cousins After All', *New Scientist*, 28.09.02; p. 20.

163. Bryant FURLOW, 'You Must Remember This', *New Scientist*,

164. Anil ANANTHASWAMY, 'Mind over Metal', *New Scientist*, 23.02.02; pp. 27–9.
165. DEHAENE, 05.07.03; pp. 30–33.
166. Michael BOND, interviewing David Attenborough, 'It's a Wonderful Life', *New Scientist*, 14.12.02; pp. 48–51.
167. See ref. 148.
168. See ref. 143.
169. See ref. 144.
170. Brian FAGAN, review of Charles Willey Pasternak, *Quest*; 'In Search of Us', *New Scientist*, 23.08.03; p. 47.
171. See refs 144 and 170.
172. See ref. 145.
173. Hemai PARTHASARATHY, 'Mind Rhythms', *New Scientist*, 30.10.99; p. 28–31.
174. AL-BUKHARI, 1994; p. 927.
175. ABBASI, 1996; p. 94.
176. AL-BUKHARI, 1994; p. 513.
177. GILLAUME, 1990, 'The Hijra of the Prophet'; p. 226.
178. John READE, Paul BROWN, Tim RADFORD, Tony ALLAN, Mark LEONARD, Jonathan WATTS and Randeep RAMESH, '2020', Part One: 'Our World in Year 2020; What Climate Change Will Do to Our Planet', *Guardian*; 11.09.04
179. Jeff HECHT, 'Vanishing Deltas', *New Scientist*, 18.02.06; pp. 8–9.
180. Curtis ABRAHAM, 'Unsettled Existence', *New Scientist*, 'Comment and Analysis', 22.04.06.
181. See refs 178, 179, 180.
182. See ref. 178; pp. 26–8.

(Continuation of ref. 163:) 15.09.01; pp. 25–7.

183. 'Destruction of Rare Species, Local People Eating Bush Meats (Africa)', BBC 1 and Channel 4 News, 2006.
184. Michael BOND, interviewing Archbishop Desmond Tutu, 'Reflections of the Divine', *New Scientist*, 29.04.06; p. 48.
185. Samuel P. HUNTINGTON, 'The West and Modernization', *The Clash of Civilizations and the Remaking of the World Order*, Touchstone Books, 1998; pp. 68–72.

Chapter Four
Philosophy: Unity and Diversity in Humans

186. See ref. 131.
187. Dan JONES, 'All About Me', *New Scientist*, 19.08.06; pp. 28–36.
188. 'The Mechanism of Immunity', *Readings from Scientific American; Immunology*, with an introduction and additional material by F. M. Burnet, W.H. Freeman and Co., San Francisco, 1976; p. 17.
189. Fazhur RAHMAN, 'Contemporary Modernism – The New Situation', *Islam and Modernity – Transformation of an Intellectual Tradition*, University of Chicago Press, 1984.
190. Ibid.; pp. 86, 87.
191. See refs 187, 188.
192. See ref. 135.
193. Bruce LAWRENCE, review of and commentary on *The Book of Signs*; 'The Quran: A Biography', *Guardian*, 'Books that Shook the World', 29.10.06.
194. Claire AINSWORTH, 'Spirit of Mendel', *New Scientist*, 29.06.02; pp. 50–53.

195. See ref. 93.
196. Hazel MUIR, 'DNA Reveals Its Talent for Computing', *New Scientist*, 26.11.94; p. 17.
197. Bennett DAVISS, 'The Computer Within', *New Scientist*, 08.01.00; pp. 18–22.
198. Melanie COOPER, 'Life 2.0 Complex Evolution', *New Scientist*, 08.06.02; pp. 28–33.
199. Philip COHEN, 'Code', *New Scientist*, 30.08.03; pp. 35–7.
200. Helen PHILIPS, 'Master Code', *New Scientist*, 15.03.03; pp. 44–7.
201. See ref. 95.
202. See ref. 96.
203. Susan GREENFIELD, 'Sensational Minds', *New Scientist*, 02.02.02; pp. 30–33.
204. Stanislas DEHAENE, 'Natural Born Readers', *New Scientist*, 5.7.03; p. 32.
205. Pete MOORE, 'A Sense of Place', *New Scientist*, 15.04.00; p. 12.
206. 'Connectome', *New Scientist*, 'The Word', 12.11.05; p. 62.
207. *Concise Medical Dictionary*, 2nd edn, Oxford University Press, 1985; p. 54.
208. Michael COLEMAN and Kate BENDALL, 'Keeping Your Nerves', *New Scientist*, 27.08.05; pp. 31–3.
209. See refs 95 and 96.
210. See refs 163 and 164.
211. Graham LAWTON and Rita CARTER, 'Let's Get Personal', *New Scientist*, 13.09.03; pp. 30–35.
212. Gail VINES, reviewing Frans de Wall, *Good Natured*, *New Scientist*, 24.05.03; p. 56.
213. See refs 210 and 211.

214. Kerri SMITH, 'For Women Food Is Food for Thought', *New Scientist*, 29.04.06; p. 17.
215. Kevin FOX, 'The Neuro Connection', *New Scientist*, 10.11.01; p. 56.
216. Max VELMANS, 'In Here, Out There, Somewhere', *New Scientist*, 25.03.06; pp. 50–51.
217. Helen PHILIPS, talking to John Allman, 'The Cell that Makes Us Human', *New Scientist*, 19.06.04; pp. 32–5.
218. Kevin LALAND and Gillian BROWN, 'The Golden Meme', *New Scientist*, 03.08.02; pp. 41–3.
219. John GRAY, 'I Think, but Who Am I?', *New Scientist*, 14.09.02; pp. 46–9.
220. Daniel DENNETT, 'Free Will but Not as We Know It', *New Scientist*, 'Human Nature'; pp. 39–40.
221. Helen PHILIPS, interviewing Alan Snyder, 'The Genius Machine', *New Scientist*, 03.04.04; pp. 30–33.
222. See refs 96 and 203.
223. See refs 211 and 212.
224. DAVIES Bennett, 'Imitation of Life', *New Scientist*, 03.12.05; p. 46.
225. See refs 223 and 224.
226. See refs 219 and 220.
227. PARTHASARATHY, *New Scientist*, 30.10.99; pp. 28–31.
228. See ref. 186.
229. Paul VALLEY, 'Modern Education Fails the Spiritual Test', The Independent, 'Editorial and Comment', 09.10.02.
230. Frans de WALL, 'The Animal Roots of Human Morality', *New Scientist*, 14.10.06; pp. 60–61.

231. Priya HEMENWAY, 'The Book of Lieh Tzu', *The Little Book of Eastern Wisdom*, Barnes and Noble, New York, 2003; p. 94.
232. Lis ELSE, interviewing Mary Midgley, *New Scientist*, 03.11.01; pp. 48–51.
233. David F. PEAT, 'Saving of Planet Gaia', *New Scientist*, 18.03.06; pp. 48–9.
234. Ibid.
235. Martin KEMP, 'Intimation and Intuition', *New Scientist*, 09.09.06; pp. 48–9.
236. Jonathan KINGDON, interviewing James Randerson, 'Out of Africa', *New Scientist*, 19.07.03; pp. 44–7.
237. Ian STEWART, 'Never Ending Story – Power of Infinity', *New Scientist*, 27.09.03; pp. 29–33.
238. EINSTEIN on 'The Mysterious' and 'The Religiousness of Science', excerpts from 'The World as I See It', last revision 18.01.99; GOOGLE search, 28.11.04.
239. Antonio DAMASIO, review of Albert Einstein, *Admiration and Influence of Spinoza's Work*; 'Mind over Matter', *Guardian*, 10.05.03.
240. Stephen HAWKING with Leonard MLODINOW, 'Conclusion – We Find Ourselves in a Bewildering World', *A Briefer History of Time – the Science Classic Made More Accessible*, Bantam Press, London, 2005; pp. 138–42.
241. Amanda GEFTER, 'Mr Hawking's Flexicurve', *New Scientist*, 22.04.04; pp. 28–32.
242. BOND, 14.12.02; pp. 48–51.
243. See ref. 229.
244. Rowell HUESMANN, 'Bad Influence', *New Scientist*, 03.04.04; p. 7.

245. Alison MOTLUK, 'Blame It on the Box', *New Scientist*, 06.04.02; p. 16.
246. *The Press*, Barnet, 09.11.06.
247. See refs 244 and 245.
248. Kate DOUGLAS, 'Evolution and Us', *New Scientist*, 11.03.06; pp. 30–32.
249. 'The Thought Detectives', *New Scientist*, 'Editorial', 22.11.03; p. 3.
250. Robin DUNBAR, 'We Believe', *New Scientist*, 28.01.06; pp. 30–33.
251. 'Meditation – Seminar and Display', Victoria and Albert Museum, 30.11.03.
252. DALAI LAMA with Frédérique HATIER, 'Karma', 'Meditation', 'Ahimsa', 'Nirvana', *The Dalai Lama's Little Book of Inner Peace*, Element/HarperCollins, 2002; pp. xvi, 107, 178, 181, 195.
253. Kate FOX, 'Religion', *Watching the English: The Hidden Rules of English Behaviour*, Hodder & Stoughton, 2005; p. 355.
254. John McCRONE, comments on Robert Jahn, 'Psychic Powers: What Are the Odds?', *New Scientist*, 26.11.94; p. 26.
255. *Concise Oxford Dictionary*, Oxford University Press, 2001; p. 1371.
256. *Oxford Mini-Reference Dictionary and Thesaurus*, Oxford University Press, 1995; p. 601.
257. *Collins Gem English Dictionary*, London and Glasgow, Collins, 1981; p. 494.
258. *The New Collins Concise English Dictionary*, London and Glasgow, Collins, 1985; p. 1106.
259. *Encarta World English Dictionary*, Bloomsbury/Microsoft/Encarta, 1999; p. 1789.

260. John Robert HINNELLS (ed.), *Dictionary of Religions*; Penguin, 1984 .
261. Ibid.; pp. 25, 307, 308.
262. Ibid.; p. 25.
263. Ibid.; p. 55.
264. Ibid.; p. 57.
265. Ibid.; p. 56.
266. Ibid.; p. 269.
267. Ibid.; pp. 26, 199.
268. Ibid.
269. Ibid.
270. Ibid.; p. 277.
271. See ref. 155.
272. See ref. 239.
273. Mark FORSTATER, 'The Meditations of Marcus Aurelius's *Cultivating the Self*', *The Times* (2), 19, 20, 24, 26, 27 April 2000.
274. Amanda GEFTER, 'The Riddle of Time', *New Scientist*, 15.10.05; pp. 30–33.
275. Klaus K. KLOSTERMAIER, 'One World of Wisdom', 'The Work of the Divine', *Bhagavata Purana – The Wisdom of Hinduism*, One World, Oxford, 2000; pp. 25, 59, 60, 63, 66–7.
276. W. OWENCOLE, 'Sikhism: Adi Granth', *Teach Yourself World Faiths: Sikhism*, Teach Yourself Books, 1994; pp. 116–23, 124, 132–4.
277. See refs 250, 251. 252.
278. R. A. LAMBOURNE, 'The Local Church', 'The Liturgical Movement', 'And the Health', *Community Church and Healing*, Arthur James, 1987; pp. 116–17.

279. Lucinda VARDEY (ed.), 'Mother Teresa', *The Book of Peace – Finding the Spirit in a Busy World*, Rider, 2002; pp. 5–25.
280. Collin Becket RICHMOND, 'Religion – Faith – Prayer', *A Collection of Shaker Thoughts*, Introduction by Eldress Gertrude, New York, 1993; p. 59.
281. Rabbi Lionel BLUE, 'Rabbiburger', Hodder & Stoughton, 1989; p. 142.
282. Prya HEMENWAY, *Sufism – Way of the Heart*, 2003; pp. 53–5.
283. John WOLFE, 'Introduction: Persistence, Pluralism and Perplexity', *The Growth of Religious Diversity – Britain from 1945*, ed. Gerald Parsons, Routledge/Open University, 1993; pp. 7–8, 11–12.
284. Ibid.; pp. 133–73.
285. Jamil SHARIF, 'Muslims in Britain; Facts and Challenge, British Muslim Demography', *British Muslim; Islamic Expo*, London, July 2006.

Chapter Five
Fulfilment: Creative Art

286. Mark HANSON, 'A Clearer Picture', *Independent on Sunday*, 09.03.97.
287. Ian STEWART, 'In the Lap of the Gods', *New Scientist*, 25.09.04; pp. 29–33.
288. H. W. JANSON, 'Introduction to Human Art', *History of Art – A Survey of the Major Visual Arts from the Dawn of History to the Present Day*, Prentice Hall, Inc., Englewood Cliffs, NJ, and Harry N. Abrams Inc., New York, 1968, p. 17.

289. Ibid.; pp. 9–10.
290. Vassily NOVIKOV, 'Introduction to Beautiful Expression and Prophet', *Artistic Truth and Dialectics of Creative Works*, trans. Eugeni Filippov, Progress Publishers, Moscow, 1981; pp. 10–15.
291. Ibid.; p. 19.
292. See ref. 285.
293. See ref. 159; pp. 169–73.
294. See ref. 15; p. 180.
295. See ref. 128; p. 20.
296. Douglas PALMER, 'Neanderthal Art Alters the Face of Archaeology', *New Scientist*, 06.12.03; p. 11.
297. HENSHILWOOD et al., University of Bergen, 'Civilisation', *New Scientist*, 18.09.04; pp. 27–8.
298. Yvonne RIDLEY, reviewing Aisha Ahmad and Roger Boase, *Pashtun Tales from Pakistan*, *Q News*, Mar.–Aug., 2003; p. 41.
299. Jonathan GOTTSCHALL, 'Fictional Selection', *New Scientist*, 03.03.07; pp. 38–41.
300. See ref. 290; p. 7.
301. Ibid.; p. 10.
302. Ibid.; pp. 10–11.
303. Ibid.; p. 14.
304. See ref. 133.
305. See ref. 287; p. 10.
306. See ref. 289; p. 14.
307. See ref. 287; p. 16.
308. See ref. 286.
309. See ref. 289; pp. 7, 8, 10, 11, 14.
310. See ref. 297.
311. See ref. 294; p. 15.

312. See refs 296 and 297.
313. See refs 300 and 301.
314. See ref. 309.
315. Eugene SAMUEL, 'What Lies Beneath?', *New Scientist*, 09.02.02; pp. 24–7.
316. See ref. 68.
317. Patricia CRONE and Michael COOK, *Hagarism – the Making of the Islamic World*, Cambridge University Press, 1980; pp. 6–7.
318. 'Muhammad', *Encyclopedia of Islam*, 1st edn, 1913–36, E. J. Brill; vol. vii, pp. 360–87.
319. See ref. 238.
320. See ref. 235.
321. See ref. 236.
322. Ben LONGSTAFF, interviewing Marcus du Sautoy, 'Maths and Music Go Together', *New Scientist*, 22.11.03; pp. 48–51.
323. David APPELL (ed.), 'Truth and Beauty Creates Maths', *Guardian*, 14.09.02.
324. Michael BROOKS, 'Dangerous Liaisons', *New Scientist*, 16.08.03; pp. 32–3.
325. Marcus CHOWN, reviewing Yurij Baryshev and Pekka Teerikorpi, *Discovery of Cosmic Fractals*, *New Scientist*, 'Books', 25.01.03; p. 52.
326. Enrico COEN, 'Way to Grow', *New Scientist*, 08.11.03; pp. 44–7.
327. Martin KEMP, 'Intimations and Intuitions; Structural Intuitions', *New Scientist*, 09.09.06; pp. 48–9.
328. Keith CRITCHLOW, 'Foreword', 'Introduction', *Islamic Patterns – an Analytical and Cosmological Approach*, Thames and Hudson, London, 1976; pp. 6, 7.

329. See ref. 324.
330. See ref. 323.
331. Jeff GREENWALD, interviewing Ned Kahn, 'Forces of Nature – Turning Art of Chaos', *New Scientist*, 16.10.99; pp. 49–51.
332. Ibid.
333. See ref. 288, 'The Ancient World'; pp. 19, 20.
334. Ibid., 'Old Stone Age', p. 22.
335. Ibid.; p. 23.
336. Ibid., 'The Ancient Near East'; pp. 50–51.
337. See ref. 159, 'Introduction, the Form – the Art'; p. xiii.
338. See ref. 288, 'The Middle Ages'; p. 189.
339. Ibid., 'Islamic Art'; p. 190.
340. Ibid.; p. 189.
341. Ibid.; p. 189.
342. Ibid.; pp. 190, 194.
343. See ref. 159, 'The Form – the Art'; p. 168.
344. William DALRYMPLE, 'The Ectasy of God's Dancers', *New Statesman*, 13.12.04; pp. 22–5.

Index

A

Acceptance 16, 43, 44, 100, 114, 128
action 33, 69, 91, 92, 97, 99, 107, 109, 120, 150
activity 5, 6, 7, 25, 42, 45, 46, 49, 58, 65, 66, 69, 70, 71, 72, 93, 95, 96, 108, 170
adaptation 30, 88, 113
adulthood 17, 19
adversity 4, 9, 16
aesthetic vii, 3, 168
age 1, 2, 3, 26, 37, 70, 80, 134, 142, 144, 145, 163, 165
agricultural 28, 89
alcohol 31, 33
Amerindian 117
Amniotic 20
anatomical 17, 22
animal 26, 45, 64, 75, 78, 79, 81, 85, 87, 89, 95, 166
anterior 22
anthropological 25, 81
ants 65, 79
apes 60, 75, 79, 87
appeal 133
arabesque 166
Arabs 1, 65, 66, 69, 127
Architectural 164
arrogance 92, 93
art 130, 132, 155, 164
art: creative 6, 13, 45, 52, 55, 57, 58, 70, 92, 131, 133, 135, 137, 168, 194

art forms 165
artifact 3
artist 3, 7, 131, 132, 133, 134, 135, 144, 151, 163, 165, 168
artistic vii, 2, 3, 7, 10, 11, 130, 131, 132, 133, 134, 135, 136, 137, 138, 140, 143, 144, 145, 153, 157, 161, 163, 164, 165, 166, 167, 168, 169, 170
artistic: idea 132, 169
Asteroids 53, 183
atmosphere 52, 53, 55, 60, 63, 78, 82, 83, 94, 113
attitude 14, 70, 82, 93, 94, 104, 106, 109, 128, 152
audience 11, 131, 132, 151
Australian 74, 117
awe 126, 131, 132, 152, 163
axons 103
aya 9

B

Backgrounds 12, 23, 72, 80, 85, 87, 88, 98, 99, 126, 127
bacterial 25, 30, 32, 87
bad 6, 15, 16, 28, 59, 61, 62, 100, 107, 108, 109, 118
balance 17, 18, 35, 38, 54, 55, 66, 73, 77, 82, 95, 96, 97, 156, 163
barley bread 29
barrier 1, 6, 44, 72, 160
beating 30
beauty 3, 5, 6, 7, 130, 131, 135, 136,

137, 138, 153, 156, 161, 162,
    163, 164, 165, 168
bees 65, 89, 90
behaviour 2, 33, 75, 86, 87, 88, 92,
    93, 99, 113
belief 4, 19, 42, 43, 46, 49, 71, 111,
    115, 116, 120, 122, 124, 125
beneficial 17, 36, 48, 49, 75, 94, 107,
    110, 127
Bible 19, 22, 29, 30, 31, 32, 33, 34,
    37, 49, 50, 52, 54, 56, 61, 65,
    66, 68, 69, 73, 78, 84, 91, 93,
    137, 173, 176
biological 18, 26, 61, 85, 87, 102, 128
biology 51
biosphere 55, 58, 64, 82
bird 45, 79, 87
birds 27, 28, 61, 65, 66, 75, 78, 79,
    83, 86, 87
blastocyst 177
blessing 84, 122
blindness 32
blood 23, 28, 29, 30, 32, 39, 55
body 11, 13, 14, 15, 16, 17, 18, 19,
    20, 22, 24, 25, 26, 30, 33, 34,
    37, 39, 40, 41, 55, 62, 100, 101,
    103, 107, 116, 117, 119, 128
boundaries 51, 69, 90, 92, 99, 112,
    116, 131, 133, 136, 163, 168
brain 13, 40, 64, 76, 77, 86, 87, 88,
    91, 99, 102, 103, 104, 107, 108,
    114, 116, 131, 136
brick 164
Buddhism 115, 121
buds 61, 79
burden 89, 96, 143, 154
burning 36
Bushmen 164

C

Calligraphy 166, 167
camel 79
cancer 31, 36
capacity 53, 71, 75, 91, 110
carbohydrate 29, 36

cattle 27, 28, 65, 79, 84, 85, 89, 93,
    95, 158
cell 20, 21, 23, 101, 107
challenge 194
character 45, 47, 64, 69, 72, 75, 134,
    135, 151, 154
cheese 29
chemical 22, 23, 25, 28, 33, 34, 60,
    62, 84, 101, 128
choice 36, 46, 47, 49, 69, 71, 91, 92,
    93, 108, 109
Christianity 4, 5, 118, 121, 166
chromosomes 24
chronicle 154
circulating 55
cirrhosis 31
Cleanliness 20, 33
climate 94
clot 10, 13, 18, 23, 25, 40
clothing 34, 110
clouds 12, 27, 84, 157, 160, 162, 163,
    164
cobweb 60, 65
coexist 66, 96, 99, 124
colour 24, 53, 63, 64, 80, 81, 88, 130,
    131, 134, 144
commercial 6
communities 1, 6, 27, 29, 35, 39, 60,
    63, 64, 65, 73, 74, 75, 76, 77,
    80, 83, 85, 86, 87, 89, 92, 95,
    97, 98, 100, 106, 109, 120, 122,
    126, 127, 128, 155, 169
community 3, 4, 11, 14, 17, 18, 20,
    28, 38, 39, 40, 43, 59, 64, 69,
    74, 75, 86, 96, 97, 99, 106, 121,
    124, 126, 143, 144, 150
competition 86, 113
compilation 9, 12, 140, 143
component 29, 36, 85
compose 5, 25, 53, 122, 158
composition 9, 24, 34, 53, 84, 101,
    128, 138, 142, 168
comprehensive 84, 99, 147
computer 108, 109
conception 13, 18, 19, 43

confidence 40, 115, 125
confused 15, 152
connection 190
conqueror 45
conscious 48, 107, 108, 109, 111, 136
constellations 82
constructive v, 3
consumerist 113
consumption 28, 29, 30
contaminated 29, 30
contemplate 47, 50, 65, 100, 101, 131, 132
contemporary v, 2, 6, 9, 44, 58, 99, 144, 169
contentment 113, 114, 115, 116, 119, 168
cornfields 79
cosmic 162
cow 177
crafts 134
crane 65
crash 57
creation 6, 10, 11, 19, 20, 21, 22, 24, 42, 46, 49, 50, 51, 52, 53, 54, 56, 57, 58, 59, 62, 70, 71, 83, 84, 91, 128, 130, 131, 134, 136, 137, 147, 153, 161, 162
creature 91, 93
creatures 2, 49, 55, 57, 60, 66, 80, 85, 86, 89, 90, 91, 93, 94, 97
credit 135
creepers 84
crime 113
cruelty 93
cucumber 29, 79
culture 1, 44, 62, 64, 72, 106, 123, 144, 156, 164, 166
cupping 36
cure 17, 35, 89
cycle 83, 177, 178

D

Dance 3
darkness 11, 12, 20, 21, 46, 53, 82, 83, 159, 163, 164

dates 29, 78, 80, 81
dawn 60, 131, 159, 164
death 2, 9, 16, 19, 24, 25, 26, 34, 36, 38, 45, 55, 57, 58, 59, 61, 62, 63, 69, 70, 71, 74, 117, 118, 127, 140, 154, 156, 157, 165
decomposition 25, 62
deed 92, 95, 119
deeds 40, 70, 92, 94, 118
delicious 107
desecration 111
design 137, 138, 140, 142, 156
destiny 63
destitute 145
determination 101, 108, 128
devotion 77, 115, 119, 135
dialogue 108, 109
diet 29, 36, 39
different 1, 2, 5, 9, 11, 12, 14, 16, 19, 21, 23, 25, 27, 32, 35, 37, 44, 45, 52, 53, 54, 55, 56, 64, 66, 68, 72, 77, 80, 81, 82, 85, 86, 87, 88, 89, 90, 96, 97, 98, 99, 100, 101, 102, 104, 105, 106, 107, 108, 109, 110, 112, 115, 117, 120, 122, 126, 128, 131, 133, 134, 137, 138, 140, 151, 157, 162, 166
digestible 30
dignity 174
discipline 40, 109, 167
disease 15, 17, 35, 36, 58, 95
display 87, 134
disposal 25, 57, 58, 157
diversity 16, 80, 120, 126, 127, 128, 129, 162
divine 44, 70, 132, 135, 140, 143, 165, 166
DNA 26, 53, 60, 87, 101, 102, 105, 183, 189
dog 79
dolphins 75
domestic 38, 43, 82, 89, 151, 156, 157
dominant 24, 47
donkey 79

double helix 101
dove 65
drawing 156
drawings 133, 161
drink 178, 179
dwelling 60, 61, 65, 66

E

Ears 94, 95, 96, 111
earth 18, 19, 22, 24, 25, 27, 50, 51, 52, 53, 54, 55, 57, 59, 60, 62, 65, 78, 80, 83, 84, 85, 90, 96, 111, 117, 125, 130, 156, 157
ease 15, 16, 35, 149
ecologists 77
Ecology 66
economic 99, 106, 126, 128
ectoderm 21
education 77, 99, 106, 112, 113, 119
egalitarian 13, 23, 76
Egyptian 117, 165
electric 103
elephants 75, 79, 87
embryo 20, 21, 23, 61
emigration 9
emotion 20, 35, 96, 101, 102, 105, 106, 152, 168
endoderm 21
endometrium 21, 32
energy 25, 31, 38, 135
enjoyment 133
enshrouded 150
enzymes 23, 30, 101
eternal 19, 113, 116, 117, 124, 126, 140, 152
events 9, 20, 26, 87, 94, 95, 133, 134, 137, 144
exceed 31, 73, 75, 94, 96
existence 2, 3, 4, 6, 28, 40, 51, 56, 57, 58, 59, 72, 82, 94, 95, 97, 116, 128, 143, 144, 152, 169
exosphere 52
explore 14, 16, 18, 37, 51, 66, 71, 76, 137, 138, 168

F

face value 105
faculty 86, 88, 91, 103, 121
failure 112
faith 4, 6, 17, 18, 39, 40, 42, 43, 71, 72, 76, 77, 101, 106, 114, 115, 116, 119, 121, 123, 124, 149, 153
false 123
family v, 10, 18, 21, 26, 37, 38, 86, 102, 144, 145
family planning 20
farmer 64
farming 27, 69
Fashioner 131, 170
fat 29, 31, 36
features vii, 23, 167
feelings 76, 98, 102, 108, 119, 131, 133
fertilization 21
fever 36
fibre 25, 79
fibrous 29
fig 78, 154
figures 166
finite 19, 42, 56
fire 57, 79
fish 28, 30, 47, 65, 66, 79, 90
flesh 21, 23, 25, 30
fly 65, 79
foetal 20, 23, 31
food 15, 20, 27, 28, 29, 30, 31, 33, 35, 36, 64, 65, 75, 86, 87, 89, 91, 107, 157
forceful 133
fountain 78
fractal 162
free iv, 46, 47, 70, 93, 107, 108, 110, 162
freedom 3, 46, 70, 90, 91, 92, 109, 113
free will 190
frontiers 1, 49, 74, 86
functional 16, 56, 103

201

fundamental 100
future 1, 12, 28, 45, 47, 56, 57, 60, 77, 82, 88, 91, 92, 94, 95, 111, 112, 113, 119, 122

G

Galenic 37
game hunting 69
gardens 79
garlic 79
gatherer 28
genealogy 26, 81
genes 26, 27, 80, 81, 87
genetic 17, 23, 24, 26, 27, 80, 81, 99, 101, 105
genome 87, 101
geographical 12, 72, 106, 126
Geology 66
geometrical 162, 166
gift 42, 88, 91
ginger 79
global v, 72, 97, 109
gnat 79
goat 79
good 6, 11, 15, 16, 26, 27, 28, 29, 31, 36, 38, 59, 61, 62, 63, 71, 82, 100, 107, 108, 109, 110, 111, 113, 118, 119, 121, 122, 123, 130, 132, 135, 136, 144, 149, 165, 167
grace 40, 100, 127, 128, 152
grains 79, 89, 141
graphic 137, 140
greedy 75, 96
grudging 92

H

Habitat 55, 59, 60, 63, 64, 65, 66, 77, 78, 82, 83, 95, 97, 164
Hadith 12, 23, 24, 29, 33, 34, 36, 40
happiness 6, 113, 114, 115
hardship 15, 16, 35, 38, 122, 123, 149, 150
harmonious 18, 38, 66, 73, 74, 77, 80, 82, 94, 95, 96, 97, 128, 169
harmony 38, 66, 75, 81, 82, 86, 89, 90, 96, 97, 112, 126
hasty 70, 92
healing 28, 35, 36, 37, 40, 121, 165, 193
health 6, 14, 15, 17, 20, 25, 27, 28, 30, 31, 32, 35, 36, 37, 40, 95, 177, 178, 193
heart 3, 34, 39, 40, 94, 95, 96, 111, 164
heartburn 36
herbs 37, 79, 156
hills 65, 78
Hinduism 117, 120, 193
histone 101
historical 8, 9, 12, 120, 133, 134, 137, 143, 144
history 29, 45, 47, 55, 77, 106, 120, 121, 133, 134, 151, 154, 164, 165, 167
HIV 95
holiday 113
holistic 14
honey 28, 29, 36, 66
horizon vi, 48, 99, 121, 123, 127, 163
horse 79
hospital 40, 180
house 34, 93, 145
humane 111
humanities 107
humanity 71, 111, 156
humble 100, 124, 131, 168
hunter 28
hymns 152

I

Ideal 181
Ijtehad 12, 43, 71
Imagination 116, 134, 136, 138
Immunology 188
impatient 70, 92
implantation 20, 23
impulse 103
independent 17, 43, 106, 145

individual 1, 3, 8, 14, 15, 17, 18, 21, 23, 28, 38, 40, 45, 49, 60, 62, 64, 69, 70, 71, 92, 97, 99, 101, 105, 108, 109, 115, 116, 118, 119, 128, 134, 141, 144, 153
individuality 62, 72, 75, 118
infant 29, 136
infection 30, 32, 36
information 30, 42, 43, 45, 46, 48, 101, 103, 134, 157
infrastructure 82, 114
ingenious 130, 131
injustice 114
insects 65, 74, 78, 79, 89
insight 42, 48, 50, 91, 143, 165
insolently 92
inspiration 42, 43, 45, 46, 47, 48, 100, 102, 103, 122, 123, 133, 149, 165
intestines 28
intoxicant 31

J

Jewish 121, 154, 176
Judaism 4, 5, 118, 166
justice vi
juvenile 113

K

Kindness 93, 94
kinship 26, 86
knowledge 1, 2, 3, 5, 6, 7, 10, 11, 12, 13, 16, 24, 25, 30, 38, 39, 40, 42, 44, 45, 46, 47, 48, 49, 50, 51, 52, 55, 58, 59, 60, 61, 62, 69, 71, 72, 73, 74, 76, 77, 86, 87, 88, 90, 91, 99, 100, 101, 102, 103, 106, 108, 110, 111, 112, 115, 119, 120, 122, 125, 126, 131, 132, 133, 135, 140, 147, 148, 149, 152, 162, 165, 170
Knowledge 11, 45, 46, 47, 48, 49, 71, 84, 91, 141, 142, 173, 182

known 4, 5, 9, 20, 23, 24, 26, 32, 43, 47, 48, 52, 54, 62, 72, 77, 78, 81, 85, 87, 88, 98, 99, 101, 143, 162, 166

L

Lamb 89
lameness 32
land marks 54, 55
language 3, 5, 11, 17, 22, 65, 80, 133, 142, 143, 146, 152, 161, 168, 169
laws 11, 44, 50, 51, 52, 54, 80, 124, 162, 169
learning 48, 90, 102, 103, 104, 106, 107, 119, 128
lecture 11, 147, 154
leech 21
leprosy 19, 36
life 1, 2, 3, 6, 10, 11, 12, 14, 15, 16, 17, 18, 19, 22, 23, 24, 25, 26, 34, 35, 36, 37, 38, 39, 40, 42, 43, 47, 49, 53, 55, 56, 57, 58, 59, 60, 61, 62, 63, 64, 65, 66, 69, 70, 71, 72, 73, 74, 75, 76, 77, 80, 82, 83, 84, 85, 87, 88, 90, 91, 92, 93, 99, 100, 106, 107, 109, 113, 114, 115, 116, 117, 118, 119, 121, 122, 123, 124, 128, 130, 131, 136, 137, 140, 141, 142, 143, 144, 145, 146, 147, 150, 151, 153, 154, 156, 157, 158, 161, 164, 165, 168
light vii, 3, 10, 11, 42, 44, 46, 48, 53, 54, 56, 58, 60, 64, 65, 83, 85, 88, 92, 103, 147, 159, 160, 167, 168, 170, 176
limited 6, 13, 35, 42, 45, 46, 47, 57, 59, 69, 70, 82, 87, 90, 91, 93, 109, 113, 132
lineage 26
literal 9, 105
liver 31, 179
location 9, 99, 144

love 4, 40, 86, 91, 92, 96, 100, 121, 152

M

Magnetosphere 52
Maker 120, 131, 170
Manifestations 135
mankind 1, 2, 5, 7, 15, 16, 18, 23, 27, 28, 35, 41, 47, 49, 59, 64, 69, 70, 83, 86, 88, 90, 91, 93, 94, 121, 125, 126, 127, 128, 135, 143, 145, 169, 170
marketing 113
match 84, 102
materialistic 2, 111
mathematical 111, 161
matriarchal 26
matrimonial 38
matters 43, 52, 55, 56, 57, 58, 71, 73, 77, 85, 90, 130, 145
maturity 1, 61, 144
me 64, 108, 109, 188
measured 84, 161
meat 28, 29, 30, 36, 66, 95
media 30, 32, 114, 133
medical 15, 16, 17, 18, 24, 25, 26, 31, 33, 37, 38, 39, 76, 81, 100, 101
medicine 6, 14, 16, 17, 18, 20, 22, 23, 30, 36, 37, 38, 40, 49, 79, 165
meditation 39, 40, 74, 77, 115, 168
Meme 190
memory vi, 87, 104
menstruation 32
mental 6, 14, 17, 18, 19, 33, 39, 92, 101, 126, 140
mesoderm 21
mesosphere 52
message 1, 8, 12, 26, 46, 66, 80, 87, 90, 115, 140
Messenger 4, 8, 11, 12, 127, 135, 143, 144, 148, 149
methods 28, 44, 51, 88, 134, 137, 143
middle path 73, 74, 85, 94, 95, 97, 170
milk 23, 27, 28, 29, 30, 33, 36, 89, 90

mind vi, 1, 2, 3, 6, 10, 11, 13, 14, 15, 16, 17, 18, 22, 27, 30, 33, 39, 40, 41, 43, 44, 46, 48, 69, 70, 71, 76, 100, 102, 103, 104, 106, 107, 108, 109, 110, 112, 113, 114, 115, 116, 118, 119, 120, 121, 123, 130, 131, 132, 133, 134, 135, 136, 143, 152, 155, 164
mineral 25
mirage 114
misfortune 92, 94, 95
mitochondrial 26
model 11, 111, 119, 137, 138, 142
moderate 1
modern vii, 2, 3, 5, 14, 16, 17, 18, 20, 26, 29, 35, 39, 40, 42, 44, 45, 51, 52, 55, 71, 72, 74, 75, 80, 97, 99, 100, 110, 113, 114, 115, 119, 136, 154, 161, 162, 163, 169
modernism 188
molecules 27, 60
money 38, 47
monkey 95
monotheistic 4, 118, 124, 166
moral vii, 18, 71, 106, 109, 110, 112, 113, 114, 115, 120
morality 99, 100, 108, 109, 113, 128, 129
mortal 6, 10, 19, 24, 42, 59, 72, 115, 116, 118, 119, 142, 156
mosque 167
moulded 22, 23
mountains 12, 54, 55, 57, 65, 66, 78, 82, 83, 84, 158, 160
Muhammad vi, 1, 2, 8, 9, 10, 11, 12, 13, 14, 19, 29, 42, 43, 44, 71, 76, 93, 111, 127, 135, 140, 143, 144, 145, 146, 147, 148, 149, 150, 151, 152, 153, 154, 155, 167, 168, 171, 174, 177, 178, 179, 181, 182, 184, 196
Muhammad: Hajj 127, 128
Muhammad: Ijtehad 12, 43, 71

Muhammad: life 1, 2, 3, 6, 10, 11, 12, 14, 15, 16, 17, 18, 19, 22, 23, 24, 25, 26, 34, 35, 36, 37, 38, 39, 40, 42, 43, 47, 49, 53, 55, 56, 57, 58, 59, 60, 61, 62, 63, 64, 65, 66, 69, 70, 71, 72, 73, 74, 75, 76, 77, 80, 82, 83, 84, 85, 87, 88, 90, 91, 92, 93, 99, 100, 106, 107, 109, 113, 114, 115, 116, 117, 118, 119, 121, 122, 123, 124, 128, 130, 131, 136, 137, 140, 141, 142, 143, 144, 145, 146, 147, 150, 151, 153, 154, 156, 157, 158, 161, 164, 165, 168
Muhammad: teaching 82, 113, 135, 143
multicultural 99
multi layered 100
muscle 25
music 3, 7, 40, 130, 133, 136, 167, 168
mystic 143

N

Nationalities 5, 72, 80, 81, 126, 127
nature vii, 3, 4, 6, 7, 10, 11, 27, 38, 50, 51, 53, 56, 60, 61, 62, 65, 70, 75, 77, 80, 82, 85, 88, 90, 92, 95, 96, 98, 99, 105, 111, 112, 113, 114, 120, 121, 122, 124, 126, 127, 131, 133, 134, 136, 157, 161, 162, 163, 164, 168, 169
nausea 33
needy 97
nerve cells 103
network 103, 104
networks 107, 162
neural 103, 104, 107
neurons 103
New 1, 3, 14, 48, 53, 63, 74, 91, 92, 103, 104, 119, 121, 122, 123, 143, 154, 157, 162
news 11, 42, 43, 46, 149

night 34, 52, 53, 60, 78, 83, 136, 158, 159
nodes 162
normal 14, 15, 16, 17, 19, 20, 30, 34, 38, 53, 69, 114
nourishment 23, 28
NSPCC 96
nucleus 101, 135
nurturing 86, 99, 120
nutrient 28

O

Obese 31
object 54, 107, 108, 133, 135
observe 74, 88, 131, 152, 162
ocean 12, 65, 83, 90, 163
Old Testament 34, 35, 37, 123
olive oil 29, 37, 79
onion 79
orchard 79
order 10, 11, 12, 15, 24, 29, 38, 39, 57, 58, 61, 62, 74, 95, 96, 101, 103, 108, 109, 130, 138, 140, 142, 154, 163, 169
organ 39, 180
organic 25
organs 21, 23, 107
originality 130, 164
orphan 145
others 8, 24, 28, 32, 48, 63, 75, 76, 86, 88, 90, 97, 98, 100, 101, 112, 120, 128, 129, 138, 162
ovum 20, 21
ozone 52

P

Painting 3, 7, 133, 144, 163, 164
pairs 25, 80, 81
palatable 27, 29, 89
particle 50, 51
past 1, 3, 29, 42, 44, 57, 72, 90, 95, 119, 133, 134, 144, 148, 151, 165
pasturage 65

pathological 19
patience 15, 106
patient 6, 14, 15, 17, 18, 36, 39
patriarchal 26
pattern 26, 29, 58, 74, 88, 131, 140, 150, 162
pelvic 21
pen 10, 13, 47, 48, 102, 165
people 2, 4, 6, 9, 14, 32, 33, 37, 38, 39, 42, 46, 65, 73, 74, 85, 86, 87, 93, 96, 98, 102, 106, 113, 114, 115, 116, 120, 124, 126, 128, 134, 137, 146, 149, 153, 154, 157, 164
perception 3, 26, 56, 64, 101, 104, 106, 110, 116, 128, 130, 136, 168
perseverance 46, 48, 101, 128
perspective v, 33, 109
phases 1, 56, 57, 58
philosophical vii, 1, 2, 3, 5, 98, 100, 105, 107, 115, 123, 128, 135, 140, 155, 157, 169
philosophic: idea 123
philosophy vii, 2, 3, 6, 8, 15, 35, 38, 44, 45, 46, 48, 58, 74, 85, 99, 106, 107, 109, 111, 112, 114, 115, 119, 123, 125, 128, 129, 136, 165, 168, 170
physical vii, 1, 3, 6, 7, 13, 14, 17, 18, 19, 20, 25, 27, 32, 33, 34, 36, 38, 40, 76, 81, 88, 92, 101, 106, 116, 117, 118, 126, 140, 164, 170
physicist 43, 45
piety 33, 48, 49, 71, 99, 111, 113, 135, 170
pig 79
plague 19, 34
planet 6, 57, 60, 62, 63, 74, 75, 97, 111
plants 6, 24, 26, 61, 63, 73, 74, 75, 76, 77, 78, 80, 82, 84, 85, 86, 87, 88, 89, 92, 94, 95, 166
poet 58, 64

poetry 3, 7, 69, 130, 136, 144
poisonous 30
pomegranates 78
poor 13, 92, 96, 97
posterior 22
poultry 27, 95
prayer 15, 29, 30, 33, 34, 39, 40, 74, 116, 121, 127, 128, 152, 167
precise 8, 50, 51, 53, 54, 84, 151, 156, 162, 169
pregnancy 20, 23, 31, 32
prejudice 20
Prejudice 31
present 1, 2, 9, 12, 17, 25, 42, 55, 63, 87, 88, 96, 122, 134, 135, 140, 144, 146, 151, 162, 164, 165, 169
preservation 20, 27
priest 14, 37
principle 3, 9, 50, 53, 117, 166
progeny 21, 101
prohibited 15, 30, 46, 122
property 51
proportion 22, 27, 52, 161, 162
psyche 17, 107
pumpkin 29
purity 29, 81, 82, 89, 90, 97, 124, 126
putrefaction 25

Q

Quails 65
quest 41, 187
Quran iii, v, vii, 1, 2, 3, 4, 5, 6, 8, 9, 10, 11, 12, 15, 16, 18, 19, 20, 21, 23, 24, 26, 27, 29, 30, 31, 32, 33, 34, 35, 38, 39, 40, 42, 44, 45, 46, 47, 48, 49, 50, 51, 53, 54, 56, 57, 58, 59, 60, 61, 62, 65, 66, 68, 69, 70, 74, 76, 77, 78, 80, 81, 82, 83, 84, 85, 86, 87, 88, 89, 90, 91, 92, 93, 96, 100, 102, 111, 123, 124, 126, 131, 132, 133, 134, 135, 136, 137, 138, 140, 142, 143, 144, 145, 146, 147, 148, 149,

150, 151, 152, 153, 154, 156, 157, 158, 161, 162, 164, 165, 166, 167, 168, 169, 170, 171, 172, 173, 176, 182, 184, 188
Quranic vii, 1, 2, 3, 5, 6, 8, 9, 10, 11, 12, 13, 14, 15, 16, 18, 19, 21, 24, 25, 27, 28, 29, 30, 32, 35, 37, 38, 39, 40, 42, 43, 44, 45, 46, 50, 52, 53, 54, 55, 56, 57, 58, 59, 61, 62, 64, 66, 69, 71, 72, 73, 74, 75, 76, 77, 80, 82, 84, 85, 86, 89, 90, 92, 94, 95, 96, 97, 98, 99, 100, 101, 102, 105, 106, 112, 115, 124, 125, 127, 128, 131, 132, 135, 137, 138, 140, 142, 143, 144, 145, 146, 147, 149, 150, 152, 155, 156, 158, 161, 162, 163, 164, 165, 167, 168, 169
Quranic: Composition 9, 24, 34, 53, 84, 101, 128, 138, 142, 168
Quranic: concept 6, 13, 16, 26, 27, 33, 37, 40, 56, 58, 64, 72, 73, 97, 98, 112, 128, 131, 165
Quranic: idea 58
Quranic: knowledge 74
Quranic: philosophy 6, 35, 38, 45, 58, 74, 85, 99
Quranic: verse 13, 32, 39, 44, 53, 55, 86, 95, 112, 164

R

Race 23, 80, 170
rain 25, 26, 27, 52, 61, 63, 78, 81, 82, 83, 84, 85, 94, 122, 160
rank 23
rate 34, 36, 57
rationalism 106
Read v, 10, 13, 18, 48, 77, 91, 102, 146, 165
realistic 85, 134, 136, 137, 151, 157, 158, 163, 168
reality 2, 3, 51, 129, 134, 136, 144, 151
reason 38, 43, 51, 71, 120

recede 52, 53, 57
record 47, 48, 54, 62, 154
reject 48
relief 6, 119
religion 3, 44, 72, 106, 111, 112, 115, 116, 119, 152, 166
representative 90
rest 10, 60, 61, 107, 113, 157, 158
resting place 60, 61, 86, 91
restores 39, 40, 49, 50
riding 27
right 3, 13, 46, 47, 71, 73, 95, 107, 110, 112, 113, 128
righteousness 93
rigor mortis 25
river 28, 78, 95
rivers 54, 55, 66
roads 54
roots 55, 83
rope 79
RSPCA 96

S

Salt 29, 34, 160
same 2, 5, 6, 8, 11, 12, 24, 32, 42, 44, 48, 52, 53, 54, 56, 58, 63, 69, 71, 72, 73, 78, 80, 81, 84, 85, 86, 87, 88, 90, 95, 97, 98, 100, 102, 104, 105, 109, 112, 115, 124, 127, 138, 144, 156, 162, 164, 166
sand dunes 65
sandy dust 57
satisfaction 130
science vii, 2, 3, 6, 16, 18, 23, 24, 25, 29, 30, 31, 35, 39, 42, 43, 44, 48, 50, 51, 55, 63, 71, 72, 74, 76, 80, 81, 88, 99, 100, 106, 107, 110, 111, 112, 114, 115, 119, 128, 133, 152, 161, 162, 170
scientific vii, 2, 6, 18, 30, 31, 35, 43, 44, 48, 49, 51, 52, 53, 55, 58, 60, 66, 70, 71, 74, 76, 80, 84, 86, 98, 99, 100, 101, 103, 105,

    110, 111, 114, 133, 135, 143,
    155, 161, 162, 169
scientific: idea 58, 161
scientific: knowledge 2, 30, 55, 58,
    99, 110, 162
scientific: philosophy 44
scientific: terms 18
scribes 9
scriptures 5, 77
sculpture 3
sea 28, 66, 69, 78, 82, 83, 84, 164
seeds 61, 79
self 1, 3, 6, 12, 14, 62, 64, 69, 72, 92,
    99, 100, 106, 108, 109, 113,
    118, 120, 128, 136, 144, 149,
    156, 168, 170
self-esteem 108, 109
selfishness 99, 113, 128
sensory 107
sequence 20, 133, 137
shadow 54
Shaker 121, 194
Shaper 131
shapes 23, 131, 162, 167
sheep 79
significant 21, 40
signs 46, 78
Sikhism 120, 193
silk 79, 166
silk route 166
sketches 133
skill 91, 104, 151
skin 19, 21, 36, 37, 81, 89
sky 12, 18, 22, 27, 50, 51, 52, 57, 61,
    65, 78, 83, 84, 85, 131, 136,
    141, 157
sleep 34, 125, 158
smith 173
smoky pulp 50, 51
society 2, 3, 4, 6, 14, 31, 38, 49, 66,
    74, 75, 87, 92, 96, 97, 98, 99,
    100, 109, 110, 112, 113, 114,
    119, 121, 124, 128, 133, 153,
    164, 170
soul 15, 16, 18, 33, 34, 40, 92, 115,
    116, 117, 118, 119, 122, 123,
    167, 168
sound 57, 88, 130, 131
source 4, 26, 43, 50, 61, 89, 92, 100,
    108, 118, 121, 131, 133, 152,
    153
space 12, 50, 51, 52, 53, 55, 56, 58,
    120, 141, 168, 181, 183
spatial arts 167
species 6, 30, 45, 47, 63, 73, 74, 75,
    77, 78, 80, 81, 82, 86, 87, 88,
    92, 95, 185, 188
speech 86, 88, 91, 103, 145, 156
sperm 20, 21
spices 37
spiders 60, 65
spirit 3, 14, 23, 42, 44, 60, 75, 91,
    117, 118, 165, 168, 176, 181,
    185, 188, 194
spiritual 1, 3, 5, 7, 14, 40, 112, 116,
    119, 127, 128, 131, 144, 146,
    166
spreading 52, 57, 149, 166
standard 2, 17, 109, 110
star 53, 57, 83, 158, 159
status 3, 4, 14, 19, 23, 47, 51, 72, 77,
    80, 88, 90, 94, 97, 99, 114, 119,
    135, 151, 161
stomach 21, 28
stone 61, 164
stones 78
story telling 11, 130, 134, 144, 151,
    156
strangulation 30
stratosphere 52
stream 28, 29, 78, 122
stress 14, 15, 38, 39, 45, 178
structural 16, 21, 137, 138, 140, 168
structure 20, 21, 26, 76, 86, 101, 108,
    114, 131, 136, 138, 140, 162,
    167
style vii, 3, 8, 9, 10, 11, 12, 13, 130,
    131, 133, 136, 137, 144, 145,
    151, 153, 156, 158, 161, 167,
    169

subjective 108, 109
sublime 133, 142, 153
subservient 90
suffering 15, 33
Sufis 70, 122, 136
superiority 48, 49, 73, 75, 77, 88, 90, 97
supermarket 113
superstition 46
Sura vii, 46, 47, 68, 138, 153, 156, 177, 184
surrounding 52, 95, 137
survival 15, 16, 27, 30, 47, 73, 75, 82, 86, 88, 89, 91, 120
swift 65
symbiotic 77, 85
symbol 4
symbolic 48, 144, 167
synapse 103
syrup 29, 89, 90
system iv, 16, 17, 21, 23, 26, 36, 39, 44, 54, 56, 66, 75, 91, 96, 101, 106, 112, 113

T

Taboos 14
talbina 36
tangible 133
Tao 110, 175
task force 108
taste 28, 80, 81, 86, 88, 103, 107
technological 17, 119
television 31
temperature 55, 60, 88
them 4, 5, 6, 8, 11, 18, 22, 23, 26, 27, 29, 35, 41, 42, 49, 65, 73, 76, 83, 85, 86, 89, 90, 93, 98, 128, 136, 139, 147, 148, 149, 153, 157, 160, 164
theology 18
theory 4, 37, 43, 44, 86, 111, 134
thermosphere 52
thickets 89
time v, 1, 2, 3, 4, 5, 6, 8, 9, 12, 13, 14, 15, 19, 23, 24, 26, 29, 31, 32, 33, 34, 36, 38, 39, 40, 42, 44, 45, 50, 51, 52, 54, 56, 57, 58, 60, 62, 65, 70, 71, 72, 74, 76, 88, 100, 110, 112, 113, 120, 132, 133, 134, 144, 146, 147, 156, 166, 168, 169
tolerance 15, 75, 99, 100, 106, 113, 127
torture 73, 75
toxins 30
traits 24, 27, 88
tranquility 40, 152, 156, 158
transgresses 92
translation 171, 172, 176, 177
transliteration 9
treatment 17, 39, 180
trees 65, 66, 78, 89, 94, 95, 141, 156
troposphere 52
trust 10, 115
truth 2, 8, 16, 19, 46, 94, 95, 96, 106, 111, 120, 126, 134, 136, 144, 146, 162
Tsunami 124
tufts 79
turtle 65

U

ultimate 7, 17, 63, 112, 114, 115, 116, 119, 132, 135, 153
unconscious 108
understanding v, 1, 3, 5, 6, 8, 10, 16, 26, 41, 44, 46, 48, 49, 63, 70, 71, 72, 74, 76, 82, 90, 99, 100, 102, 105, 107, 109, 111, 112, 113, 114, 127, 128, 137, 147, 170
unity 98, 120, 123, 124, 125, 127, 128, 162
universe 11, 18, 44, 50, 51, 52, 53, 57, 58, 82, 106, 110, 120, 127, 130, 132, 152, 161, 162, 169
unknown 30, 48, 50, 51, 52, 56, 57, 111, 112, 122, 152, 163
untouchable 19, 32
us vii, 6, 11, 12, 14, 15, 16, 18, 22,

26, 30, 31, 32, 34, 35, 42, 44, 47, 49, 50, 53, 55, 56, 60, 61, 63, 69, 70, 71, 74, 76, 81, 82, 85, 88, 89, 96, 97, 98, 99, 100, 101, 102, 104, 107, 108, 109, 110, 111, 113, 114, 115, 121, 122, 124, 125, 128, 130, 133, 134, 136, 137, 144, 151, 152, 153, 155, 156, 158, 165, 170, 179
useful 17, 36, 46, 78, 79, 127, 130, 132, 135, 136, 147, 165, 167
uterine 20, 21, 23

V

Vacuum 55
valuables 90
variability 99, 107
variations 80, 81, 100
variety vii, 8, 28, 32, 34, 55, 63, 72, 80, 103, 111, 116, 122, 123, 127, 133, 137, 165, 169
Vedic 40
vegetation 25, 26, 61, 63, 84, 85, 89
verify 42, 43, 46
vibration 57
vinegar 29
vineyards 78
virtual 109
virtue 120
virtuous 76
visible 47, 48, 53, 55, 133
vision 86, 88, 91, 99, 103, 153, 156, 161, 169
vitamins 29
vomiting 33

W

Walls 28, 34
water 12, 18, 22, 27, 28, 29, 33, 37, 51, 53, 55, 61, 63, 64, 66, 78, 82, 84, 85, 93, 94, 157, 180
watermelon 29
whales 75

wholesome 85, 89, 90
wind 52, 65, 78, 83, 84, 122
wine 33, 79
wings 85, 162
wisdom 1, 22, 88, 90, 100, 106, 115, 120, 122, 146, 147, 149
womb 11, 20, 23, 32, 141
wonder 14, 126, 131, 132, 136, 152, 154
wood 79, 94, 164
woods 79
words 1, 2, 5, 6, 21, 22, 29, 36, 40, 45, 47, 48, 66, 71, 86, 87, 94, 99, 104, 109, 114, 118, 128, 130, 131, 132, 134, 135, 138, 144, 147, 152, 157, 158, 161, 162, 163
worship 119, 125, 145, 152, 165
write 91, 146
wrong 3, 46, 47, 71, 107, 110, 113, 180

Y

Yoga 40

Z

Zorastrianism 117

Printed in Great Britain
by Amazon